CHEVROLET'S MODERN PERFORMANCE CAR

CAMARO

2016

LARRY EDSALL

motorbooks

Dedication

For Scott Settlemire, known throughout the Camaro community as the "F-bodfather,"
who retires confident that his beloved Camaro is in very good hands, and for those who
even now are at work on the seventh-generation car.

Quarto is the authority on a wide range of topics.

Quarto educates, entertains and enriches the lives of
our readers—enthusiasts and lovers of hands-on living.

www.quartoknows.com

First published in 2016 by Motorbooks, an imprint of Quarto Publishing Group USA Inc.,
400 First Avenue North, Suite 400, Minneapolis, MN 55401 USA.
Telephone: (612) 344-8100 Fax: (612) 344-8692

quartoknows.com
Visit our blogs at quartoknows.com

Motorbooks titles are also available at discounts in bulk quantity for industrial or
sales-promotional use. For details contact the Special Sales Manager at
Quarto Publishing Group USA Inc., 400 First Avenue North, Suite 400,
Minneapolis, MN 55401 USA.

10 9 8 7 6 5 4 3 2 1

ISBN: 978-0-7603-4981-6

Acquiring Editor: Zack Miller
Project Manager: Jordan Wiklund
Senior Art Director: Brad Springer
Cover Design: Juicebox Designs
Interior Design: Simon Larkin
Layout: Rebecca Pagel

Printed in China

General Motors trademarks are used under license to Quarto Publishing Group USA Inc.

CONTENTS

ACKNOWLEDGMENTS

The author has many people to thank for their help with this project, but none more than Tara Stewart Kuhnen, an account supervisor for MSL Group, who got stuck with the assignment from the communications staff at Chevrolet to be my advocate on this project when it came to talking with the right people at GM Design, Chevrolet Performance engineering, at the Lansing Grand River assembly plant, and in securing nearly all the photographic and other images in this book on the sixth-generation Chevrolet Camaro.

Thanks to Monte Doran of Chevrolet Communications for selecting Tara for the assignment, and to Tara for her patience with the author and his repeated requests. Thanks also to Mike Albano, head of the Chevrolet Communications team; to Tom Read, GM Powertrain Communications manager who has helped with several previous book projects; Erin Davis, the communications manager at Lansing Grand River; Pamela Flores of GM Design; and to Randy Fox and others on the GM and Chevrolet communications team.

Also to the Camaro's chief engineer Al Oppenheiser, Ed Welburn's Design team and to others at GM who shared their time with me for interviews. They include Al himself on several occasions, as well as Tom Christensen, Ara Eckel, Bill Goodrich, Ameer Hader, Jim Kalahar, Jim Karlavage, Mike Katerberg, Hwasup Lee, Jordan Lee, Aaron Link, Tristan Murphy, Bill Nichols, Dan Nicholson, Tom Peters, Besy Philips, Cheryl Pilcher, Todd Rooney, Dave Smith, Mark Stielow, Mike Trevorrow, Rich Scheer, and Ryan Vaughan. Also Mike Green of USA Local 652.

Much of the photography came from Steve Fecht and his team.

Thanks also to everyone involved in the logistics of the Find New Roads Trip, and to the team at Motorbooks/Quarto Publishing.

INTRODUCTION

"Find New Roads" is more than an advertising slogan, the latest in a long line that includes "See the USA in a Chevrolet," "Baseball, Hot Dogs, Apple Pie and Chevrolet," and "The Heartbeat of America." More than a mere motto or even a memorable advertising theme, "Find New Roads" has become the mantra, the guiding precept for the Chevrolet Division of General Motors.

Or, as Chevrolet's global brand chief and nearly 40-year GM veteran Alan Batey put it, "Find New Roads is our North Star."

Turning words into action, Batey insisted, includes ingenuity and innovation in everything Chevrolet does—in design, in performance, and in technology. But there's

The sixth-generation Chevrolet Camaro is ready to provide a way for drivers to "find new roads." *GM*

Above: Alan Batey, president of General Motors North America, applauds the launch of the sixth-generation Chevrolet Camaro at the car's unveiling on Detroit's Belle Isle. *GM*

Opposite top: Clay models (top) are used during the vehicle design process, often with different styling details on the left and right sides, so they can be reviewed in full scale. A silver-colored plastic covering provides the model with a more finished appearance. *GM*

Opposite bottom: Still wearing camouflage, a 2016 Chevrolet Camaro is driven around the Belle Isle race track (bottom left) but the cover is off for the official unveiling of the car (bottom right). *GM*

"CHEVROLET, ITS PEOPLE, AND ITS PRODUCTS . . . IMAGINE POSSIBILITIES AND SHATTER PERCEPTIONS."

even more to the quest, he said, because to qualify as a true Chevrolet, even stunning design, performance, and technology must be delivered with quality and value. From Cruze to Corvette and from Colorado to Silverado, Chevrolet vehicles must be reasonably priced yet deliver more than what's expected.

Chevrolet, its people, and its products, Batey added, imagine possibilities and shatter perceptions.

That certainly happened when, after an eight-year hiatus, Chevrolet brought the Camaro, its so-called modern muscle car, back to the automotive marketplace for the 2010 model year. To design, develop, and produce that fifth-generation Camaro, General Motors leveraged its global reach and capabilities. As a result, and boosted by the car's starring role in the *Transformers* movie, the Gen 5 Camaro attracted so many buyers it was the bestseller in its category for five consecutive years. And perhaps just as significant for Chevrolet was the fact that 63 percent of those buyers were newcomers to the brand, a figure that might have been even higher except that some people attracted to dealerships by the new Camaro ended up driving home in other Chevrolet vehicles.

Nonetheless, there was little time for the team of Camaro planners, designers, engineers, and marketing staffers to celebrate the car's success. Even as the new Camaro was rolling toward production, General Motors was going through the temblor of bankruptcy proceedings. And there would be aftershocks, especially for the Camaro crew: not long after that sensational new Camaro hit the highways and byways—and the racetracks—work began on its successor, the sixth-generation of the car.

For any vehicle development team, "next" means "new and improved." But not only would the team creating the Gen6 Camaro be tasked with improving on a stunningly successful market and performance leader, it would have to do so within the revised realities of the new General Motors. Those realities included:

- A different platform on which to base the new car
- A different assembly plant in which to build the new car
- An expanded—and perhaps controversial—range of engines to meet the demands of a rapidly changing global automotive marketplace

As if that wasn't going to be challenging enough, the sixth-generation Camaro also needed to fulfill the expectations of longtime Camaro enthusiasts as well as those who only came to know and to appreciate the car in its most recent iteration. More than that, this next Camaro had to appeal to other potential buyers whose choice included not just the Camaro and its archrival, the Ford Mustang, but also an expanding array of sporty coupes and convertibles being produced by automakers around the world.

The task would be daunting. For the team creating the sixth-generation Chevrolet Camaro—the team challenged with improving on the best of the breed—the challenge wouldn't be just to find new roads, but to do so without losing its way in the process.

DRAWING THE ROAD MAP

"We started production of the fifth-generation Camaro in March of 2009 and we were already looking at the sixth-generation possibilities," said Al Oppenheiser, a 30-year GM engineering veteran. He had been through this before, the launch of a new vehicle and work on its annual updates, in addition to planning for its next-generation successor.

Oppenheiser had overseen the development of the Camaro concept car construction that was unveiled at the North American International Auto Show in downtown Detroit in January 2006. Later, after vehicle executive leader Gene Stefanyshyn and chief engineer Doug Houlihan and their team turned the concept into a production vehicle, Opperheiser was selected as chief engineer to launch that fifth-generation Camaro into production, to develop its ensuing annual updates and special versions, and to lead the program team that would produce the car's sixth-generation successor.

Al Oppenheiser, sixth-generation Camaro chief engineer. *GM*

As successful as the fifth-generation Camaro's launch was going, the team had no time to celebrate. After all, they were still hard at work creating the ZL1 and Z/28 versions of the just-launched Camaro while they started planning for the new car's successor.

Oppenheiser didn't know how many roadblocks stood between him and that sixth-generation Camaro. As it turned out, he and the team encountered significant obstacles in rapid succession.

A New Camaro

In April 2009, the national price of unleaded gasoline topped $4—not a good sign for those working on high-performance vehicles that tend to swallow rather than sip fuel. By June, General Motors had entered bankruptcy proceedings. It was in this same time period that Oppenheiser was called to GM's global architecture design studio where GM management informed him the next-generation Camaro would be built on a different platform than the recently launched car. Oppenheiser even was shown some preliminary sketches and a mock-up of Design's vision for the next-generation Camaro—coupe bodywork atop Cadillac's smaller Alpha vehicle platform.

"This is going to be the sixth-generation Camaro," he remembers being told.

Oppenheiser saw one obvious and major problem: the car in the sketches didn't look like a Camaro. But where he saw an obstacle, he also recognized an opportunity. (The same thing—potential obstacle turned opportunity—would occur again later when the decision was made to build the new Camaro in a different assembly plant, one that had never done a convertible model, an important part of the Camaro lineup.)

But at least management was ready to extend the Camaro's life beyond the fifth-generation car. For another, while Cadillac's Alpha architecture was smaller, it was also

> "AS SUCCESSFUL AS THE FIFTH-GENERATION CAMARO'S LAUNCH WAS GOING, OPPENHEISER KNEW HE AND THE TEAM HAD NO TIME TO CELEBRATE."

A 2016 sixth-generation Chevrolet Camaro SS convertible. *GM*

lighter, which could go a long way toward enhancing any car's potential performance.

"We were looking to cut costs, the need to reduce the number of architectures," Oppenheiser added. "The next-generation Camaro gave us the opportunity to study if there was another option."

Designing Around the Roadblocks

The fifth-generation Camaro wasn't built on the traditional F-body chassis that various iterations of earlier Camaros and the Pontiac Firebird had used and updated over the years. Instead, the Camaro's comeback rode in a unique version of what GM termed its global Zeta passenger car architecture. This was a platform originally developed for use on such rear-wheel-drive cars as the Commodore SS, a sporty sedan produced by GM's Australian subsidiary Holden, and, for the North American market, the Pontiac G8, a four-door road rocket in its GXP form.

If there was a drawback to Zeta 2, it was mass, weight overcome by big, powerful engines. Meanwhile, GM also had developed another rear-drive platform. This one was called Alpha. Somewhat smaller and considerably lighter than Zeta, Alpha was created as the structure underpinning the Cadillac CTS and ATS sedans.

"Alpha was the logical choice," Oppenheiser said. "We saw the opportunity right away to start with a lighter weight platform."

The challenge would be to apply Alpha's advantages while remaining faithful to the Camaro and Chevrolet brand values, including iconic design cues and dynamic capabilities—and to do so at an affordable price point.

There was another roadblock: GM was doing away with "mule" vehicles, the earliest version of prototypes traditionally used to sort through early major development issues. Instead, designers would have to rely on computer simulations.

Fortunately for the Camaro and for its enthusiastic customers, whether longtime owners of multiple cars or those for whom the generation-five car was their first, the team had allies in Mark Reuss, a GM engineering veteran who had recently been promoted to senior product development director (and later to president of GM North America), and in GM Design, where Camaro passions are as deep as they are within the car's engineers. Together, they held firm that, as Oppenheiser phrased it, "We had to make this next car a real Camaro."

Outside Salt Lake City, Utah, a 2016 sixth-generation Camaro continues the Find New Roads tour. *GM*

This meant they had to lengthen the Alpha dash-to-axle length to retain the Camaro's iconic proportions—long hood/short rear deck—the aggressively angled windshield, and strong C-pillar. Such things, Oppenheiser noted, "defined" Camaro. They also had to widen the platform's track width, a vital factor in staying true to the Camaro's dynamic capabilities. Oppenheiser and Tom Peters, leader of the Camaro design team, were determined not to widen the car simply by bolting on wider wheels and tires, a technique he considered to be cheating the car and its customers.

Over the course of the next year, engineers and designers worked to "grow" the Alpha architecture without adding mass. One solution was widening the track through the use of longer suspension components. Another occurred when designers insisted on 20-inch wheels, which not only enhanced the car's look but its performance envelope. Next was "wall walks," Oppenheiser's term for the twice-a-week (and often well beyond the usual workday) meetings in a design studio, where sliding whiteboards showed in detail every section and joint and component of the Alpha architecture. These meetings helped engineers and designers consider whether a standard Alpha component could be retained, or whether a new Camaro-specific part was needed; in either case, they were able to determine the best ways to make those parts both strong and light.

One example: threaded bolts often have more threads than are needed to safely and securely attach a part to the car. Often, those extra threads simply extend a bolt well beyond its nut. But that just adds unnecessary weight. What if those extra threads were eliminated? Eliminate even an ounce from enough bolts and you save pounds of weight.

Back up the "wall walks" with millions of hours of computer analysis on 140 engineering models, in addition to selecting the right materials and the latest in manufacturing technologies, and you should be able to build a car that is stronger and stiffer but also

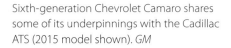

Sixth-generation Chevrolet Camaro shares some of its underpinnings with the Cadillac ATS (2015 model shown). *GM*

To keep the long hood / short rear deck proportions of classic Camaro, Oppenheiser and the GM design team lengthened the Alpha platform's dash-to-axle length. They also widened the platform's track in order to preserve the performance capabilities of Camaro. *GM*

lighter and still affordable. (Such "wall walks" have since been adopted for many other vehicle development programs at GM.

"We could make this work," Oppenheiser was convinced, but he still fretted: "We hadn't built one [car] yet."

To verify that the process actually worked, the team was allowed to build an engineering development vehicle (EDV)—the sort of vehicle GM engineers previously termed a "mule." But this test vehicle would be mounted on a four-post dynamometer, a computer-controlled testbed/torture chamber to put the car through more than a lifetime of shake and shimmy, wear and tear, simulating everything from a daily commute to the roughest of roads to fast laps around a racetrack.

Afterward, Oppenheiser knew that not only could this design work, but "we can do a great car."

His confidence increased when Aaron Link became Camaro lead development engineer. In February 2013, Link and his group based at the Milford Proving Ground found a way to take the EDV and turn it into a drivable car, an old-fashioned mule that would provide computer-generated numbers as well as seat-of-the-pants driving feedback.

The EDV looked like a compact, four-door Cadillac ATS with a lengthened hood, flared fenders, and a wider track.

"Even that car was really good right out of the box," Link said.

Oppenheiser said that, except for its taller roof height, the car "felt like a two-door sports car."

There was a lot of work ahead, for sure, but Oppenheiser was more than optimistic.

"There were obstacles that could have derailed the program," he said. "But instead, they just focused the team more on the car, on doing what was right for the car, for the Camaro."

> "THE EDV LOOKED LIKE A COMPACT, FOUR-DOOR CADILLAC ATS WITH A LENGTHENED HOOD, FLARED FENDERS, AND A WIDER TRACK."

CHAPTER TWO

EARLIER ROADS

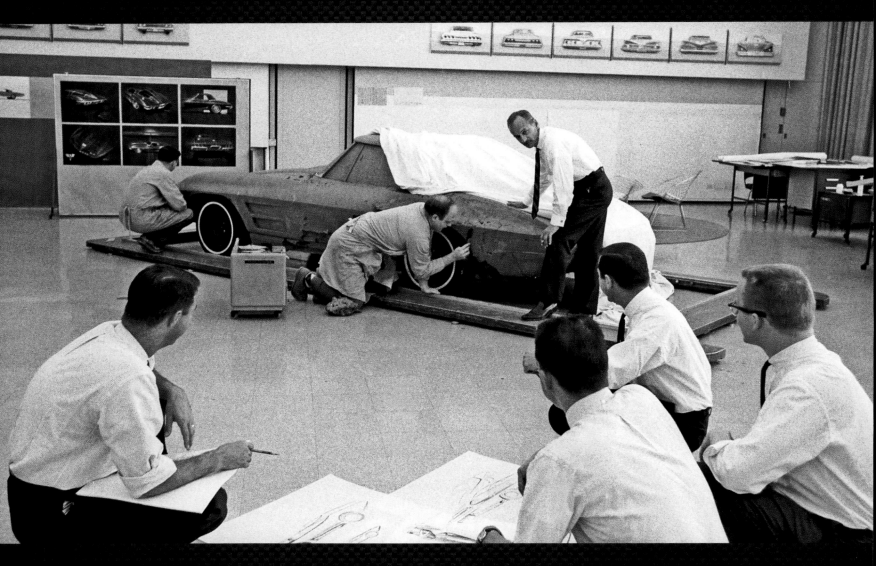

Irv Rybicki (standing beside the left rear quarter panel of a clay model of the 1963 Chevrolet Corvette and leading a discussion among a group of GM designers) pushed for a small, junior version of the Buick Riviera. The car would evolve into the original Chevrolet Camaro. *GM*

The rearview photograph of the clay model shows the official project designation—XP-436—and the unofficial name for the car—Panther. *GM*

At the New York Auto Show in early April 1964, Chevrolet unveiled a concept car it called the "Super Nova." Though built over the compact Chevy II concept car platform, this stunning concept looked nothing like an economy car, instead appearing like the beautiful offspring of a marriage between Chevrolet's own Corvair and Buick's new Riviera. It was sleek and stylish—but not available for purchase: "It was just a concept piece to see what reaction we'd get from the public, and the reaction was fairly good," Irv Rybicki, Chevrolet's chief designer, remembered. "The car looked a lot like an 8/10s-scale Riviera and featured a hardtop roof flowing smoothly back into the fenders through knife-edged sail panels that bracketed the rear deck lid."

The American car-buying public was hungry for just such a car. Any doubts about that were put to bed a few weeks later at another New York City venue—the World's Fair—where Ford unveiled its new Mustang model, the car launched an entire automotive genre.

The "Super Nova" project derived from Rybicki's initial reaction to the new Riviera model, introduced by Buick for the 1963 model year. As a specialty car, the Riviera was a luxurious vehicle designed around personal dimensions and featuring a sporty

"GENERAL MOTORS FINALLY HAD A REAL COMPETITOR TO GO UP AGAINST FORD'S THUNDERBIRD."

appearance. General Motors finally had a real competitor to go up against Ford's Thunderbird, the highway cruiser that had evolved from a small, two-seat roadster.

By designing and developing a smaller version of the Riviera—sort of a "Riviera Junior"—Rybicki thought GM could offer an even sportier coupe through the company's Chevrolet dealerships. In 1962, he approached his boss, Bill Mitchell, General Motors vice president of design, about creating such a car. Mitchell, a sports and race car fan and champion of the Corvette Sting Ray, liked Rybicki's idea and approved preliminary design work. His approval was contingent on the work being kept secret until the shape was set and a clay model of the car was ready to be shown to GM executives.

This new coupe would be based on the platform already serving to underpin the compact Chevy II economy car. In this variation, though, modernized brakes and suspension would provide a much more sporting, dynamic capability, in keeping with the car's dynamic appearance.

A secret design studio was set up in a warehouse across the road from GM Design, then as now housed within the expansive, campus-style grounds of the GM Technical Center in Warren, Michigan, a northern suburb of Detroit. It took five months for Rybicki's Riviera Junior to progress from sketches to clay model. Only then did he invite Chevrolet's new general manager, Semon "Bunkie" Knudsen, to take a look.

Knudsen reportedly liked what he saw, but canceled the project: he knew that such a car would hurt sales of the new, midsize Chevelle, which Chevy planned to roll out for the 1964 model year. Plus Chevrolet already had the Corvette and the sport compact Corvair.

Officially, Rybicki's Riviera Junior project was abandoned, though it wasn't forgotten. Late in 1963, Rybicki had Hank Haga and his Chevrolet Number Two Studio go to work on a project what would become the Super Nova concept car. Again, Knudsen liked the car, and this time he tried to figure out a way to get the rest of General Motors' management to consider it for production.

"Jack Gordon was president of the corporation, and he was not very excited about sporty cars," Knudsen later recalled. "He turned us down on Super Nova."

As it turned out, though, Gordon's voice wasn't the final word on the subject. While working on Rybicki's Riviera Junior and Haga's Super Nova, GM designers had no idea that their counterparts at Ford were busy on a similar project, designing a sporty coupe based on a compact economy car chassis.

In Ford's case, the platform came from the Falcon. The car that would gallop off that humble base into automotive glory was unveiled at the 1964 New York World's Fair—and on the cover of both *Time* and *Newsweek*—as the original "pony car": the Ford Mustang. By the time General Motors was able to take the Super Nova idea from design concept to production vehicle, Ford sold over a million of its Mustangs.

In August 1964, the GM board of directors approved XP-836, the official internal code name for what Chevrolet designers and engineers called the Panther project. And the

"IN AUGUST 1964, THE GM BOARD OF DIRECTORS APPROVED XP-836, THE OFFICIAL INTERNAL CODE NAME FOR WHAT CHEVROLET DESIGNERS AND ENGINEERS CALLED THE PANTHER PROJECT."

The 1967 Camaro Z28 shared many design cues with the original 1964 full-scale model (opposite). *GM*

Chevrolet dealers gather in the ballroom of the Book Cadillac Hotel in downtown Detroit for their introduction to the 1967 Chevrolet Camaro. *GM*

car might have gone to market as the Panther had it not been for Ralph Nader, the lawyer-turned-author.

Nader was working for Assistant Secretary of Labor Daniel Patrick Moynihan as well as serving as advisor to the U.S. Senate Subcommittee on Automobile Safety. In 1965, Nader published *Unsafe at Any Speed*, a book that opened with a chapter entitled "The Sporty Corvair—The One-Car Accident." The Corvair had been Chevrolet's original compact car. Unlike those produced by other Detroit automakers, it had the flair of an exotic Italian or German sports car, including an engine mounted behind the passenger compartment.

In light of public reaction to Nader's book, GM management deemed the name Panther simply too aggressive for Chevrolet's sporty new car. Gemini, Colt, and Chevette were considered as alternate names, until Chevrolet Merchandising Manager Bob Lund and Ed Rollet, a GM vice president, discovered "Camaro" while going through decades-old foreign language dictionaries. Camaro, they read in *Heath's Standard French and English Dictionary*, published in the 1930s, meant "friend," "pal," or "comrade."

Friend—what better name to give a new car designed to provide personal transportation with a fun and sporty flair?

20

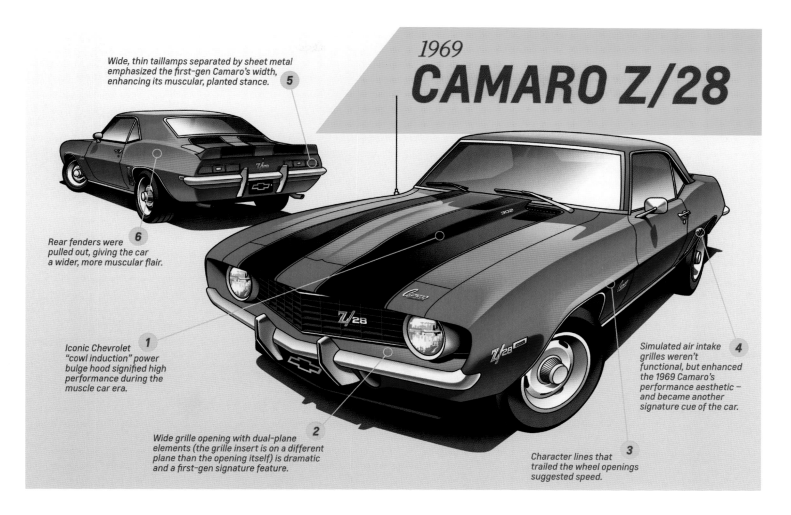

1969 **CAMARO Z/28**

Wide, thin taillamps separated by sheet metal emphasized the first-gen Camaro's width, enhancing its muscular, planted stance. **5**

Rear fenders were pulled out, giving the car a wider, more muscular flair. **6**

Iconic Chevrolet "cowl induction" power bulge hood signified high performance during the muscle car era. **1**

Wide grille opening with dual-plane elements (the grille insert is on a different plane than the opening itself) is dramatic and a first-gen signature feature. **2**

Character lines that trailed the wheel openings suggested speed. **3**

Simulated air intake grilles weren't functional, but enhanced the 1969 Camaro's performance aesthetic – and became another signature cue of the car. **4**

Graphic shows styling cues for the first-generation Chevrolet Camaro. *GM*

"This [name] suggests the real mission of our new automobile—to be a close companion to its owner—tailored to reflect his or her individual tastes and at the same time provide exciting personal transportation," Chevrolet General Manager Eliot "Pete" Estes said at the car's introduction to the automotive media on June 29, 1966. "Chevrolet has chosen a name which is lithe, graceful, and in keeping with our other names beginning with 'C' . . . . It suggests the comradeship of good friends . . . as a personal car should be to its owner."

Camaro Gen 1

General Motors launched sales of the 1967 Chevrolet Camaro on September 12, 1966, and six months later GM offered a second version of the car, the Firebird, sold through Pontiac dealerships.

The team led by Henry Haga developed the Camaro's Coke-bottle sculpting and other exterior design details, while its interior accoutrements came from George Andersbach and his stylists; its dynamic capabilities were generated by an engineering enterprise directed by Don McPherson. Though they started with the basics of the new chassis for

A 1967 Camaro Z/28. *GM*

the 1968 Chevy II, McPherson and company made extensive changes. The Camaro was the first General Motors vehicle with a separate subframe to cradle the engine, and it was also the first created with computer simulation to assist in developing parameters for the suspension system.

Significantly, the Camaro had a wider stance than the Mustang and was an inch longer and slightly lower in overall height than its rival.

Available as a coupe or convertible in Sport Coupe or Super Sport (SS) trim, Camaros could be optioned with a special Rally Sport (RS) appearance package that brought hidden headlamps, parking and backup lights grafted into the front or rear valences, and other cosmetic enhancements.

The standard engine for this early version of the Camaro was a 230-cubic-inch inline six-cylinder that pumped out 140 horsepower. Also available was a 250-cubic-inch six that offered 155 horsepower. Since nearly three-quarters of first-year buyers opted for V-8 engines, though, the most common version seen on the road was either a 327-cubic-inch unit rated at 210 horsepower or a 327 tuned to provide 275 horsepower.

Meanwhile, the Super Sport (SS 350) carried a 350-cubic-inch V-8 that took the power rating to 295 horsepower. Just before the end of calendar year 1966, Chevrolet added a SS 396 version. That car came with a "big-block" 396-cubic-inch V-8, providing 325 horsepower (and a Posi-Traction rear axle to help keep that power under control). In May 1967, a Camaro SS 396 convertible served as the pace car for the 51st Indianapolis 500-mile race.

During the Camaro's first model year, a 302-cubic-inch V-8 with 290 horsepower also became available. This special version of the car, known by the unusual moniker of Z/28, was named for the alphanumeric used in the Chevrolet options ordering system.

Ford's Mustang and Mercury Cougar, General Motors' Camaro and Pontiac Firebird, Chrysler's Plymouth Barracuda and Dodge Challenger, and American Motors' Javelin represented versions of the new and sporty pony car genre. In response, the Sports Car Club of America (SCCA) offered those cars a place to race, first incorporating the category into the American Road Race of Champions and then creating a new professional

"GENERAL MOTORS LAUNCHED SALES OF THE 1967 CHEVROLET CAMARO ON SEPTEMBER 12, 1966, AND SIX MONTHS LATER GM OFFERED A SECOND VERSION OF THE CAR, THE FIREBIRD, SOLD THROUGH PONTIAC DEALERSHIPS."

1970 **CAMARO Z28**

Chevrolet-signature dual taillamps convey beauty through simplicity. **5**

Sail panel area is surprisingly complex in the way it flows to the rear of the car, contributing significantly to the lean aesthetic. **6**

Bold split-bumper design with RS package creates a bold, aggressive and more contemporary appearance – and is a signature design cue. **1**

Hood with excellent form flows seamlessly with the distinctive split-bumper front end. **2**

Strong horizontal crease from front to rear creates tension in the body that accentuates the car's lean, muscular proportion. **3**

Lower portion of the body below the crease tucks in to expose the tires, enhancing the muscular stance. **4**

Graphic shows styling cues for the second-generation Chevrolet Camaro. *GM*

racing series, the Trans-American Sedan Championship. Almost immediately, the series was known simply as the Trans-Am. Soon after, this name became so popular with motorsports fans that Pontiac applied the name to the high-performance version of its Firebird, paying the SCCA a fee for each car that carried the badging.

Regulations restricted cars racing in the Trans-Am series to 5.0-liter (305-cubic-inch) engines. This presented a couple of challenges for Chevrolet. For example, under the terms of an American Automobile Manufacturers Association agreement, Detroit automakers had vowed not to participate directly in motorsports competitions. To get around this rule, they had to find creative ways to encourage (and fund) private racing teams to use their products. A further complication: GM didn't have an engine that was competitive and fit the 5.0-liter limit.

Both challenges were overcome by Vince Piggins. Piggins had been chief engineer of the "Fabulous Hudson Hornets" that dominated Southern stock car racing in the

"FOR THE CAR'S SECOND GENERATION, GM DESIGN DIRECTOR MITCHELL PUSHED FOR A MUCH MORE EUROPEAN LOOK ... MANY CAME TO CONSIDER THE SECOND-GENERATION CAMARO TO BE THE WORKING MAN'S (OR WOMAN'S) FERRARI."

A 1968 Camaro SS. *GM*

early 1950s. He moved over to General Motors just as Chevrolet was launching its "small-block" V-8. Working through the Nalley Chevrolet dealership in Atlanta, Piggins established the Southern Engineering and Development Company (SEDCO) as a way for Chevrolet to field what were basically factory entries in NASCAR racing. SEDCO fielded six specially built and exotically equipped 1957 Chevrolet 150 sedans that became known as "Black Widow" Chevrolets. Powered by fuel-injected engines with 283 cubic inches of displacement (cid), the cars won races, sometimes finishing 1-2-3. But the effort was short-lived, as Congress pressured Detroit to pull out of racing, in part because politicians believed it encouraged reckless driving on public highways.

To get the Camaro into Trans-Am racing, Piggins, at this point manager of Chevrolet's product promotion department, maneuvered vehicle marketing money into a racing budget. With his team, he devised Regular Production Order (RPO) Z/28, an option that included stiffer springs and anti-roll bars, quicker steering gears, rear-disc brakes (from the Corvette), a stronger rear axle, a larger fuel cell, and a modified engine.

To create the 302-cubic-inch displacement engine, Piggins' group took the Camaro's 327-cubic-inch engine block and inserted an upgraded version of the crankshaft from the 283-cubic-inch V-8 that powered the Chevy II Nova SS. The high-compression engine was also equipped with special pistons, camshaft, an intake manifold topped by a Holley dual-feed carburetor, and an exhaust system that featured less restrictive mufflers.

Bolt on a good set of tires and you were ready to go racing, which is just what happened. The first Z/28 went to Chevy dealer and racing team owner Roger Penske, who ordered some race-prep enhancements from legendary racing mechanic Henry "Smokey" Yunick. The car was slated to be driven by the soon-to-be-famous Mark Donohue.

Donohue dominated the 1968 Trans-Am racing season, winning 10 of 13 races and helping to launch one of the racing history's most famous dynasties—and one of the most famous automotive option codes.

But Piggins and team were far from finished. While the Z/28 proved to be great for most high-performance applications, getting serious power required an even larger engine, something like the 427-cubic-inch ZL-1 that was available in late 1960s Chevrolet Corvettes. For 1968, the ZL-1 could be ordered for the Camaro, but only through the

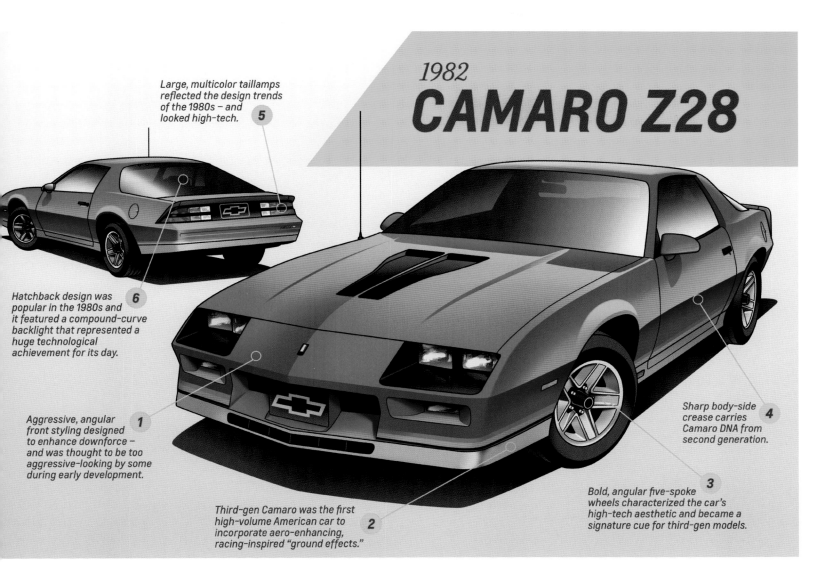

1982
CAMARO Z28

Large, multicolor taillamps reflected the design trends of the 1980s – and looked high-tech. 5

Hatchback design was popular in the 1980s and it featured a compound-curve backlight that represented a huge technological achievement for its day. 6

Aggressive, angular front styling designed to enhance downforce – and was thought to be too aggressive-looking by some during early development. 1

Third-gen Camaro was the first high-volume American car to incorporate aero-enhancing, racing-inspired "ground effects." 2

Sharp body-side crease carries Camaro DNA from second generation. 4

Bold, angular five-spoke wheels characterized the car's high-tech aesthetic and became a signature cue for third-gen models. 3

Graphic shows styling cues for the third-generation Chevrolet Camaro. *GM*

backdoor method of employing the company's Central Office Production Order (COPO) system designed for cars sold to special fleets, such as police departments. Offered through special dealers to special customers, the so-called COPO Camaros provided blistering performance potential on American drag strips.

The Camaro went through annual updates, and each of the early cars has become cherished among classic car collectors. Then, for the 1970 model year, the car underwent a ground-up, generational change with significant alterations instead of minor annual facelifts and equipment updates.

Gen 2

For the car's second generation, GM design director Mitchell pushed for a much more European look, to the point that many came to consider the second-generation Camaro to be the working man's (or woman's) Ferrari.

But as popular as the car may have been, a strike at the Norwood, Ohio, assembly plant, an oil crisis, toughening emission laws, a push for vehicle downsizing, and even new federal bumper regulations combined within a few years to threaten the Camaro's continued production. Indeed, Ford shrank the Mustang into the Mustang II for 1974. Chrysler pared the Dodge Challenger and Plymouth 'Cuda, and AMC soon eliminated the Javelin altogether.

The Camaro continued, though it wasn't spared from the cutbacks. The SS model was eliminated. In its place, a Type LT (for Luxury Touring) joined the lineup. It wasn't until the 1977 model year that the Z/28 would return, and then with a mere 170 horsepower.

As if these developments weren't bad enough, some within General Motors wanted to switch the Camaro from its sporty, rear-wheel-drive "F-body" architecture and base it instead on the front-wheel-drive platform used for the Chevrolet Citation sedan. Such a move would have changed the car's dynamic appeal, and it would have eliminated the possibility of providing a V-8 engine.

Graphic shows styling cues for the fourth-generation Chevrolet Camaro. *GM*

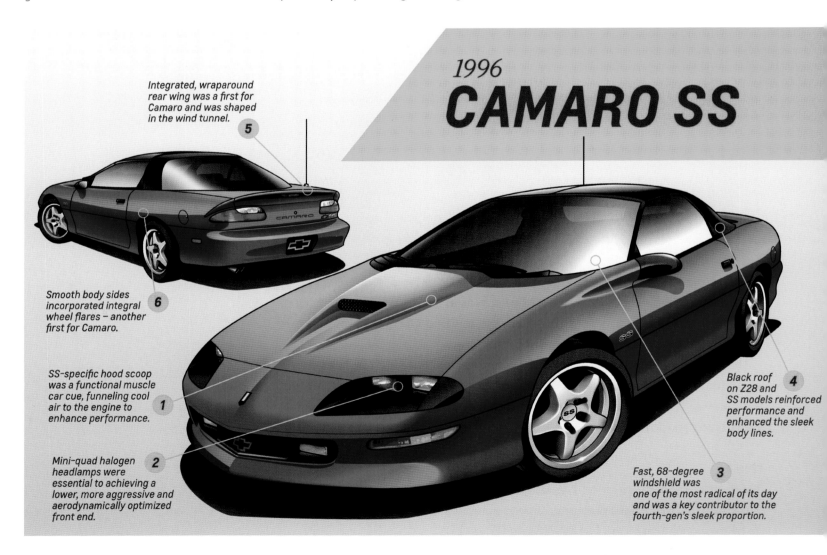

1996
CAMARO SS

Integrated, wraparound rear wing was a first for Camaro and was shaped in the wind tunnel.
5

Smooth body sides incorporated integral wheel flares – another first for Camaro.
6

SS-specific hood scoop was a functional muscle car cue, funneling cool air to the engine to enhance performance.
1

Mini-quad halogen headlamps were essential to achieving a lower, more aggressive and aerodynamically optimized front end.
2

Black roof on Z28 and SS models reinforced performance and enhanced the sleek body lines.
4

Fast, 68-degree windshield was one of the most radical of its day and was a key contributor to the fourth-gen's sleek proportion.
3

Gen 3

Despite such threats, work on the third-generation Camaro began in 1975, though it wasn't until the 1982 model year that the car would reach the road, fortunately with its power still reaching the road through the rear wheels. The body was again redesigned (Rybicki had succeeded Mitchell as head of GM design), featuring a rear window that was among the largest and most complicated pieces of automotive glass ever devised.

With Ford's Mustang also returning to its roots, the race was on again. Camaro got a boost via the IROC-Z, a special version of the Z/28 that became the basis of the International Race of Champions, a popular motorsports series that featured champions from various styles of racing competing in identical cars.

In 1987, a convertible version of the Camaro became available for the first time in nearly 20 years. The following year, a special 1LE version was devised to meet the needs of those racing in the SCCA and other showroom stock categories.

But just as the road was opening up for Camaro, there was another strike. Sales slumped. The Camaro was aging, yet third-generation production run would stretch more than a decade. Again, the car's demise was rumored, or at least talk of switching to a front-wheel-drive platform was heard. This change would most likely turn the car into a two-door version of the Chevrolet Lumina sedan.

Once again, however, the Camaro contingent within General Motors pushed on.

Gen 4

The fourth-generation car began production in 1993, though with production moved to Sainte-Thérèse, near Montreal in eastern Canada. In this new plant, the car was built with a sleek new body and some weight-saving plastic body panels, though there was a yearlong delay for a convertible version. Nonetheless, the Z/28 came with a Corvette's 350-cubic-inch V-8 engine, tuned to provide 275 horsepower, 15 less than in the sports car. There was a new 1LE package as well, and, in 1996, racer Ed Hamburger and his Street Legal Performance (SLP) tuning shop worked with Chevrolet to bring back the Camaro SS. SLP set up its own facility at LaSalle, Quebec. In this arrangement, Chevrolet built the cars and SLP tweaked them to generate 305 horsepower.

Things may have seemed fine, but the car's chassis was based on old technology. New federal safety regulations were coming, with regulations that would demand

"ALTHOUGH IT WOULD BE AN EIGHT-YEAR HIATUS, THE FIFTH-GENERATION CAMARO WOULD DO MUCH MORE THAN MERELY REVIVE THE CAMARO NAMEPLATE."

The SS version of the fifth-generation Chevrolet Camaro, which was reborn for the 2010 model year after an eight-year hiatus. *GM*

a major investment to update the car's architecture, something General Motors was not willing or able to make. There were too many other priorities, both for car buyers and automakers. As General Motors vice-chairman and car guru Bob Lutz would later explain, the F-body platform beneath the Camaro and Firebird had become "a bridge too far in bad packaging."

Insiders knew as early as 1996 that the Camaro was done (although production would run until the summer of 2002). There was almost no money for the usual model mid-generational lifecycle update, and workers retiring from the plant in Sainte-Thérèse were not being replaced. GM's powerful pony car was being allowed to atrophy.

Supported by email messages from Camaro enthusiasts, with printouts reaching some four feet in height, the F-body faithful within GM tried to resuscitate the car.

"We started work on the car a couple of times unofficially," said Scott Settlemire, son and grandson of Chevrolet dealers and a longtime GM product planner and marketing staffer who became known as the "F-bodfather" to the greater Camaro owners community. Settlemire revealed that one effort to save the car was code-named Paragon, while another looked at raiding the Corvette and Cadillac CTS parts bin as the basis for a new (though much more expensive) Camaro.

Still another variant was the GMX280, was essentially an effort to use the Australia-built Holden Monaro as the basis for a new Camaro. (The effort didn't work as a Camaro, but it did eventually lead to the Monaro's use as the basis for a new Pontiac GTO.)

"We got caught each time," Settlemire said of the projects, which were pursued for as long as possible in secret.

Actually, he said, it was a good thing such efforts were halted, because neither the timing nor the product would have been right. The new Camaro, a car he was confident would be built—someday—needed to be a car not cobbled together but one that truly lived up to its hallowed nameplate. Although it would involve an eight-year hiatus, that fifth-generation car would do much more than merely revive the Camaro nameplate.

"Let's Do a Camaro!"

In the late winter of 2004, Ed Welburn, vice president Global GM Design, took charge of the update. A few months earlier, Welburn had hired Bob Boniface, a former Chrysler designer, to work in GM's advanced design studio. The future of the Camaro came up while on their way home from the Geneva Motor Show.

"How's it going?" Welburn asked Boniface.

"Pretty good," Boniface replied.

"Can you think of anything you might want to work on?" Welburn asked.

"I want to do a Camaro," Boniface replied.

"Don't start with me," said Welburn, remembering that much of his initial conversation with Boniface involved talk of the Camaro, a car both of them grew up owning.

"I'm not telling you not to work on it," Welburn said. "But if you do, just don't let anyone see it."

Boniface and another design manager, Brian Smith, had plenty of work on Buick and Cadillac concept vehicles to keep them busy. Over the course of the summer, and with no fanfare, they also created a three-eighths clay model of a potential Camaro-style coupe. This version was designed for GM's Zeta platform, a rear-wheel-drive chassis used primarily in Australia and initially targeted to carry a new rear-drive Chevrolet Impala sedan as a challenge to Chrysler's successful full-size 300.

That Impala didn't happen, but Lutz, pushing to take advantage of GM's global strengths, helped Pontiac import a modified Holden Monaro coupe, badged as a new Pontiac GTO, from GM's Australian subsidiary. In April 2005, designers in Michigan set out to see if a car recognizable as a Camaro could be built on the Holden platform. At the same time, their boss, Welburn, went to the meeting where six top GM executives would decide on concept cars for the following year's auto show circuit.

"Let's do a Camaro!" Welburn said just 10 minutes before that meeting was scheduled to end.

"A Camaro hasn't been on anybody's radar," said Oppenheiser, whose current duties included overseeing concept car construction.

According to Welburn, the room got real quiet.

But he got the nod to create a Camaro concept. Boniface and his group would refine their car. Another group, led by GM veteran Tom Peters, who had just finished the sixth-generation Chevrolet Corvette, would work on an alternative proposal, one that would push the Camaro design envelope into the future.

" 'I'M NOT TELLING YOU NOT TO WORK ON IT,' WELBURN SAID, 'BUT IF YOU DO, JUST DON'T LET ANYONE SEE IT.' "

SANGYUP LEE

This is Sangyup Lee's initial sketch for what would evolve into the 2010 Chevrolet Camaro. *GM*

The Camaro concept was unveiled January 9, 2006, at the North American International Auto Show in downtown Detroit. At least for the moment this gave people something to talk about other than the company's financial losses and whether it was destined for bankruptcy. In August of that year, GM announced that the Camaro would go from concept to production vehicle. Much of the development work would be done in Australia, where a team of engineers from Warren (GM Tech Center) and Milford (GM Proving Ground) had been transplanted to oversee revisions to what had become the company's global rear-wheel-drive platform as it was adapted for the various vehicles on which it was built.

Gen 5

Among those vehicles would be the new fifth-generation Camaro, launched as a 2010 model, ending the eight-year gap in Camaro production. In addition to V-6 and V-8 cars and RS and SS models, the fifth-generation car would mark the return of a Camaro convertible and of ZL1, Z/28, and COPO powertrain packages.

This new Camaro proved popular even before it went into production. In the summer of 2007, the car had a leading role in the *Transformers* movie, a film in which a clapped-out 1976 Camaro transforms into the Camaro-concept-based Bumblebee character, which helps save the movie's hero and heroine—as well as the entire planet Earth—from the evil Decepticons.

The movie introduced the Camaro to a new, younger generation. When the car arrived in Chevrolet dealer showrooms, it was an immediate hit, outselling the rival Ford Mustang for five years in a row through the spring of 2015.

Dual-element taillamp design is a timeless Chevrolet cue.

5

Rear-fender kick-up feature evokes first-gen heritage and adds muscular character to the fifth-generation design.

6

Cross-car, dual-plane grille is a heritage cue reimagined for the fifth generation, giving the car a sporty character.

1

Power bulge hood is reminiscent of the "cowl induction" hood offered on the first-gen Camaro.

2

Camaro-signature sharp body-side crease returns, adding sculpture to the design.

3

Rear fender "gills" are a homage to the signature cue of the 1969 Camaro.

4

Graphic shows styling cues for the fifth-generation Chevrolet Camaro. GM

"WHEN THE CAR ARRIVED IN CHEVROLET DEALER SHOWROOMS, IT WAS AN IMMEDIATE HIT, OUTSELLING THE RIVAL FORD MUSTANG FOR FIVE YEARS IN A ROW THROUGH THE SPRING OF 2015."

Styling may attract people to the Camaro, but the car's
performance has to live up to the design's promise. *GM*

The highly revised interior of the 2016 Chevrolet Camaro. *GM*

"Nobody has to have a Camaro."

So says Cheryl Pilcher, whose job is to make sure that each Camaro has everything the customer wants. Pilcher is the Camaro's product planning manager.

She was also the head product planner for the fifth-generation Camaro. She moved to the marketing staff after nine years as a vehicle engineer at General Motors Milford Proving Ground, where she was involved with the third- and fourth-generation F-body cars. Her first duties in marketing were as assistant product planner on the Chevrolet Corvette, followed by work with the internal group that sought to resurrect the Camaro.

"As you might guess," she said, "we're always thinking ahead. Even as we have a new car coming out, we're thinking, 'This is great, but what are we going to do to make it better?'"

"We know how to make a great Camaro," she added. "We just need to find the recipe to make the car better and better and better."

"STYLING IS FIRST. THEN COMES PERFORMANCE."

According to Pilcher, it starts with design:

We've outsold Mustangs for the last five years. As you spend time with your enthusiasts and look at data on recent purchases, very consistently exterior styling pops to the top. It's always key to have something new and something fresh. It has to be attractive, not just new. It has to be something that people fall in love with. People fall in love with the car and they don't want anything else. There are lots of cars. You want somebody to fall in love, and styling is so critical.

In the sports car segment, she said, a car appears long in the tooth after five or six years, and she hinted that work is already beginning on a seventh-generation Camaro.

So styling is first. Then comes performance.

"It's a rear-wheel-drive sports car. There has to be the element of horsepower and 0 to 60 times, something that allows you to have the bragging rights," she said.

"But beyond that, it has to be fun to drive, to drive all day long."

Part of that all-day driving pleasure involves the car's interior:

We didn't get much critical acclaim on the fifth-generation interior. The sixth-generation is fabulous. It's tons better. Everything you touch feels good. And the sound is right. That's another component people want. They want the car to sound good. Induction. Exhaust. With windows up or down.

And on top of that there's the refinement. People want bragging rights. 'Cool stuff in my car.' When I bring my brand-new Camaro home and show it to my next-door neighbor, what am I going to brag about?

Full Customization Options

In the sixth-generation car, Pilcher said, those features include the 24-color ambient lighting system, the infotainment system, the reconfigurable display screen, selection options for different driving modes—snow and ice, touring, and track—and the capability to change the vehicle's volume: "I can make my exhaust note louder or quieter."

"There's so much personalization and that rings the bell for these customers, that mine is set up for *me*."

Regardless of the engine and transmission in a given car, buyers can personalize their sixth-generation Camaro. Within a few months of launch, the basic engine will be a

Below: Graphic shows the various settings that result from using the Driver Mode Selector control in the sixth-generation Chevrolet Camaro. *GM*

DRIVER MODE SELECTOR

	Snow/Ice	Tour	Sport	Track (SS only)
Electronic throttle progression	SNOW/ICE	NORMAL	NORMAL	TRACK
Automatic transmission shift map	NORMAL	NORMAL	SPORT	TRACK
Automatic transmission Performance Algorithm Shift	N/A	N/A	AVAILABLE	AVAILABLE
StabiliTrak – Competitive Driving and Launch Control	N/A	N/A	AVAILABLE	AVAILABLE
Electric power steering calibration	TOUR	TOUR	SPORT	TRACK
Engine sound management (dual-mode exhaust)	STEALTH	TOUR	SPORT	TRACK
Magnetic Ride Control calibration (if equipped)	TOUR	TOUR	SPORT	TRACK
Ambient lighting (if equipped)	ICE BLUE	BLUE	RED	ORANGE

2016 CAMARO PERFORMANCE

2016 Camaro Coupe	Transmission	0-60 mph (seconds)	1/4-mile (ET @ mph)	Max Lateral (g)	60-0 Braking (feet)
2.0L Turbo 18" AL3 tires	manual	5.4	14.0 @ 100	0.85	129
	auto	5.5	14.0 @ 99		
1LT WRS V6 20" RF3 tires	manual	5.2	13.7 @ 102	0.89	124
	auto	5.1	13.5 @ 103		
1SS V8 20" RF4 tires	manual	4.3	12.5 @ 115	0.97	117
	auto	4.0	12.3 @ 116		

Above: Graphic shows performance numbers generated during Chevrolet's internal testing of the 2016 model year Chevrolet Camaro with its various powertrains. Enthusiast magazines are generating even quicker acceleration numbers in their early evaluations of the car. *GM*

turbocharged 2.0-liter four-cylinder, but owners of the car can ride on leather seats.

"For a standard engine, it's going to be a quick and fast car with lots of torque," Pilcher said. "And then the V-6, with 60 more horsepower, that's healthy, and that will be our optional engine. But we're not going to force you to buy all the bells and whistles to get the V-6."

Speaking of that four-cylinder turbo, Pilcher said, "It's been interesting for our team to watch the sports segment and how it's been accepting of such an engine. We didn't necessarily know that four or five years ago."

Al Oppenheiser, the Camaro's chief engineer, admits his eyes were opened when he saw what the turbocharged four-cylinder engine offers, both in performance and in prospective sales. Younger buyers in particular have come to accept boosted four-cylinder engines in imported cars.

With the lighter and tighter sixth-generation Camaro, kids who watched the *Transformers* and have been transformed into car buyers can get their own Camaros. They can purchase whatever they want, even vehicles with a turbocharged four-cylinder engine that scoots to 60 miles per hour in less than 5 1/2 seconds but also provides better than 30 miles per gallon in fuel economy.

Sure, nobody *has to* buy a Camaro—but GM's incredible design team has made deciding to buy the sixth-generation car a lot easier.

"IT HAS TO BE FUN TO DRIVE ALL DAY LONG."

Cheryl Pilcher, shown in a fifth-gen Camaro convertible, brought nine years of GM engineering experience to Corvette and Camaro product planning. *GM*

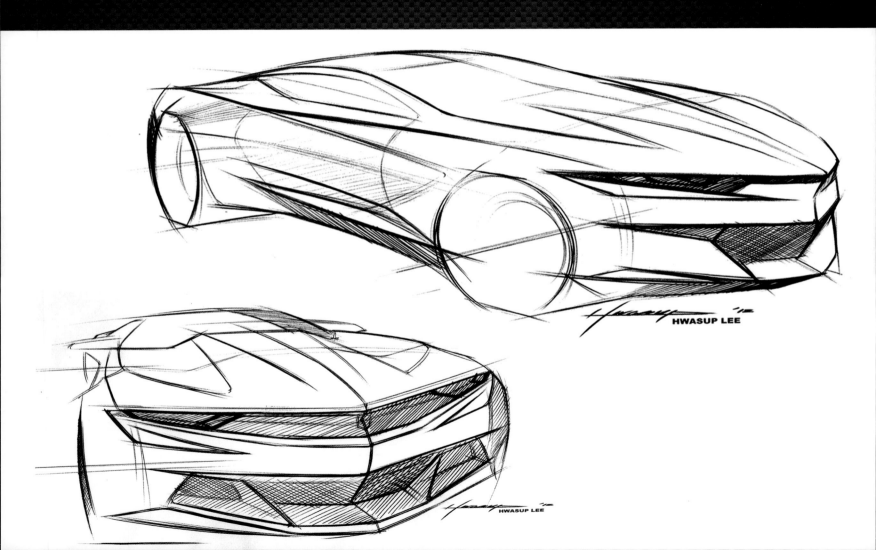

HWASUP LEE

HWASUP LEE

Work began on the design of the Chevrolet Camaro's successor not long after its introduction in the fall of 1966. This doesn't mean a 1968 model to follow that original 1967 version, but an all-new, second-generation Camaro that the public wouldn't see until the 1970 model year.

"In those days," then-Chevrolet General Manager Pete Estes told engineer-turned-author Gary Witzenburg, "we felt that four years was about as long as we dared go with anything." Actually, Estes said, the desired automotive lifecycle should span only three years, "so we started working on a new Camaro immediately after the '67 was announced."

Ford already had more than a million-car head start with the Mustang it had launched in 1963, and Chevrolet was tired of playing catch-up.

"So we said that this second Camaro has got to be the ultimate," Estes continued as he detailed the list of engineering changes, updates, and improvements for the second-generation car. "We [also] said it had to be the most beautiful automobile we have ever designed."

What Estes and GM design leader Mitchell wanted was a car that would be sort of an affordable Ferrari or a working person's Corvette. Corvettes were available in the design studio for inspiration, but so was a Ferrari 275 GTB.

The result was a second-generation Camaro that was much different in appearance from the original model. Fenders and hood were more pronounced. The grille was taller

Above and following pages: Various designers submitted preliminary and subsequent drawings as the design theme for the sixth-generation Chevrolet Camaro was developed. *GM*

Hwasup Lee. *GM*

VISIONS
OF
CAMARO

CASEY SWANSEGER

BRIANMALCZEWSKI | 13

HWASUP LEE

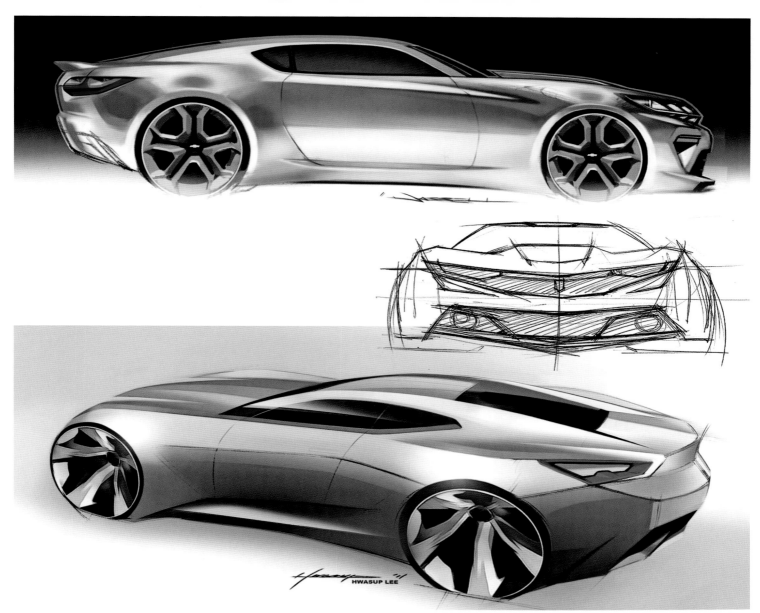

HWASUP LEE

GONZALEZ

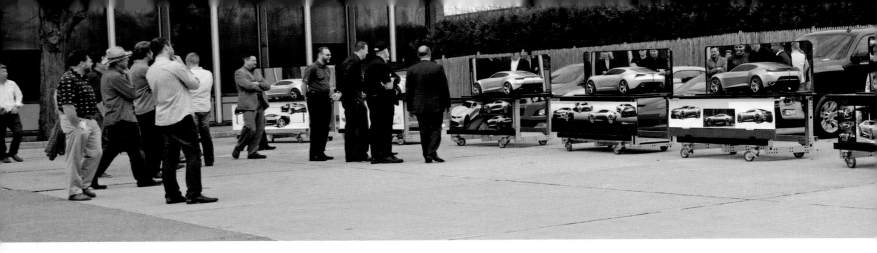

Above: In March, 2012, various drawings and clay models of proposed sixth-generation Chevrolet Camaros went through a preliminary screening by GM Design leaders. *GM*

Right: Tom Peters (in hat) and Ed Welburn study sketches and a clay scale model proposed as a possible sixth-generation Chevrolet Camaro. *GM*

and narrower, split by a thin bumper on the standard model but splitting what became a pair of smaller bumpers beneath the more prominent headlamps on the RS version. The C-pillar or "sail panel" was more complex in shape, and the roof was reminiscent of a fastback. There was a crease down the side of the car and tires were more exposed to underscore its more athletic, sporty look.

New Designer, New Designs

When he sat down to start sketching what he hoped would become the 2016 Chevrolet Camaro, Hwasup Lee experimented with drawings inspired by that second-generation Camaro's grille. But GM Design had been involved with the car's development even before Lee and others started drawing.

"Our first Design opportunity was to modify an already great Alpha architecture to achieve the dramatic proportions of what we felt delivered a Camaro," said Rich Scheer, Chevrolet Performance Car studio and Camaro design manager who with studio head Tom Peters was very involved in those early modifications. Scheer is a GM Design veteran of more than twenty years who has worked on various vehicles and in studios on multiple continents. He was a leader of a skunkworks effort to keep the Camaro from going out of production when the fourth-generation car had run its course.

"Camaro proportions are short front overhang, long powerful hood, long dash to axle, high belt line, low roof, short deck lid, wide track, large diameter wheel and tires," Scheer added. "Once these elements were in place, we had the canvas for the next Camaro."

"Leaner and meaner," Scheer said of the opportunity the new platform provided. "Lean Muscularity" would become the name of the surfacing or form vocabulary that would evolve as the shape and details of the sixth-gen Camaro emerged.

As usual, GM Design chief Ed Welburn opened the styling of the new Camaro to proposals from staffers in all of GM's studios around the globe. "Ultimately it came down to two proposals," said Peters, "Hwasup Lee's from the Warren Performance studio and the other from the California studio." He added, however, "the Camaro's success is based on excellent blend of experienced talent and diverse culture backgrounds with blended knowledge to naiveté. Ultimately, the team of designers, ranging from the most seasoned to right out of school, including Rich Scheer, Kirk Bennion, Scott Wassell, Hwasup Lee, Casey Swansager, Brian Malczewski, Adam Barry, and many other talented designers and sculptors."

Peters noted that Chevrolet's "Lean Muscularity" form vocabulary is personified in "an elite athlete who is as strong as he is fast," and is enabled by everything from aerodynamics and packaging technology engineering to GM body-panel stamping technology.

"You will find in the sixth-gen design there is much more filleting and transition from one surface to the next. Shapes are bold and taut but flow from one surface to the next.

Some were chosen to be produced as full-size clay models for further exploration of possible styling themes. *GM*

Cover a clay model in a special plastic fabric and it looks like a real car. *GM*

"WHILE LOOKING TO THE FUTURE, AS DESIGNERS MUST DO, LEE BRINGS A STRONG APPRECIATION FOR THE STYLING HISTORY OF THE VARIOUS GM BRANDS."

"One of the ways that the 2016 Camaro is easily recognizable is the front-end graphics, the cross-car shape that connects the headlamps and surrounds the upper grille opening. We used new technology for the headlamps to make the upper slot even narrower and this allowed the lower grill opening to increase. The narrow eyes and the large mouth add to the aggressive street fighter nature. By opening the lower grille this provided more air flow, better engine cooling which provides improved performance.

"Certainly, throughout the design process we explored many alternative ideas," he added, "including versions that looked at the second-gen split bumper front. All were exciting, but this front immediately said 'Camaro.'"

Hwasup Lee had been lead exterior designer on the seventh-generation Chevrolet Corvette Stingray and ultimately would hold that same title on the sixth-generation Chevrolet Camaro. However, his proposals for the Camaro would be judged the same as everyone else's.

Lee is a native of South Korea and moved to the United States while in high school. He attended the Art Center College of Design in Pasadena, California, and joined GM after his graduation.

While looking to the future, as designers must do, Lee brings a strong appreciation for the styling history of the various GM brands. He also likes to experiment boldly, exploring a variety of options in his early sketches and drawing inspiration from iconic GM models. For example, his early sketches in the competition to design the seventh-generation Chevrolet Corvette harkened back to the historic Corvette SS racer.

Soon after joining GM, Lee designed the 2001 GMC TerraCross concept, working in advanced design studios in the United States and England. After doing yet another concept for GMC, he developed an early design proposal for Cadillac and was chosen to be lead exterior designer for what would become the Buick Encore and Chevrolet

Trax. In 2008, while working in the GM Performance Cars studio and designing the ZL1 version of the fifth-generation Camaro, Lee submitted sketches for the seventh-generation Corvette. Not only were his sketches chosen to be the basis for the new car, but Lee was selected as the lead exterior designer of the stunning new Stingray. Next he was chosen to lead the exterior design team for the next Camaro.

"My first sketches [of the next Camaro] did not have the single-slot aperture grille," said Lee, who based those sketches in part on the second-generation Camaro design.

But even Lee had second thoughts when he considered his work. He realized that there were many sporty coupes already in the marketplace with such tall and less-than-full-width grilles and, with the exception of the second-generation version, the wide and single-aperture grille design had been "owned" by Camaro throughout the decades. He also realized that, for many people, the Camaro introduced as a 2010 model was their first Camaro; it had reset the standard for Camaro both for new and former owners. The car was already iconic, and it made sense to use that car as the starting point for the next one, though not in a way that would constrain the design effort.

"We own this," Tom Peters, director of GM Performance Car design, said of the wide-aperture grille. "You should look at a car without any graphics on it and know exactly what it is. If you do your job right, the car is the logo, the car is the brand."

In August, 2012, full-scale clay models are evaluated in a walled-off courtyard at the GM Styling Dome in Warren, Michigan. *GM*

Lee explained that the goal was "to build on the success" of the sixth-generation car while building the next Camaro on a new and significantly lighter, somewhat smaller underlying platform. Therefore, while retaining "Camaro identity," the new car could be "more expressive, more sculptural and more function-driven," Lee said.

In fact, while the "big forms" may look familiar and definitely indicate from a distance that the car is a Camaro, the only carryover parts from the previous car's exterior are the SS badge and the Chevrolet bow-tie emblem on the rear deck lid.

"Everything else is new," Lee said. "It has more athletic gesture, more motion to the body side, an all-new light signature—front and rear—and new graphics . . . a more precise look that represents the vehicle's improved capability."

Above: Tom Peters may be the head of Chevrolet Performance design, but he's a hands-on leader, here checking the fine points of a full-size clay model. *GM*
Below: GM's West Coast advanced design studio also gets its crack at refining the Camaro design. *GM*

"The surface vocabulary of the new Camaro is more sculptural and expressive with a lot of detail you can see and feel," added Tom Peters, director of GM Performance Car design. "As wonderful as today's Camaro is, this one takes it up to another level . . . beautifully powerful and functionally serious. We've learned from listening to performance customers and our racing experience has enhanced the serious nature of this car."

One factor that supported such changes was the new platform.

"We had an opportunity to do a new architecture and we had no problem with that," said Peters. "You just felt that it was the right thing to do intrinsically."

Peters said the new platform opened opportunities for form vocabulary, new technology, and performance improvements. You come in with your eyes wide open and accurately identify the areas you need to pursue.

"Just like with music," he said. "You can come up with something fresh and new. You may put in some heritage spice and consistency of the brand, but there are infinite variations."

Kirk Bennion, who heads GM Performance Car exterior styling, had worked together with Peters and Lee on the seventh-generation Corvette. In that venture, they were joined by Ryan Vaughan, whose sketches formed the basis for that car's interior; he headed the interior design team of the Corvette project as well as taking over interior design for the sixth-generation Camaro. According to Peters, the Corvette showed them ways to design for certain features—including proportions, sculptural quality, and dramatic sectioning—that could be applied to the Camaro's new taut platform.

He added, though, that "the [Camaro's] proportions are so unique and different [from Corvette]. There were some things we could translate through a Camaro filter, but nothing direct. There's a Corvette sensibility and there's a Camaro sensibility, and from my standpoint, it's easy to keep them separate."

On Camaro, he said,

There's part of the muscle car proportion, a certain amount of visual heft or power in the front of the car between the cowl and the front end and a certain amount of visual mass that has to go there to have that tall, muscular form, and you have to have the wheel diameter to support that. Likewise with the fenders and quarters. You have to have a big wheel/tire graphic to support those shapes. The team did a really good job. We didn't compromise anything.

Tom Peters, head of Chevrolet Performance design. *GM*

"YOU SHOULD LOOK AT A CAR WITHOUT ANY GRAPHICS ON IT AND KNOW EXACTLY WHAT IT IS. IF YOU DO YOUR JOB RIGHT, THE CAR IS THE LOGO, THE CAR IS THE BRAND."

By October, 2012, things are getting serious with the design, as evidenced by all the suit coats in the room. *GM*

GM Design head Ed Welburn studies a Camaro proposal in late October, 2012. *GM*

Tom Peters considers two proposals in November 2012. *GM*

Above: GM Design executives consider alternative styling proposals for the sixth-generation Camaro in November 2012. *GM*

Below: GM Design leadership takes a closer look at one of the full-scale proposals. *GM*

A fifth-generation Camaro provides perspective when considering a possible sixth-generation proposal. *GM*

" 'JUST LIKE WITH MUSIC,' HWASUP LEE SAID, " 'YOU CAN COME UP WITH SOMETHING FRESH AND NEW. YOU MAY PUT IN SOME HERITAGE SPICE AND CONSISTENCY OF THE BRAND, BUT THERE ARE INFINITE VARIATIONS.' "

We had discussions about do we just throw everything out and do totally new, like with the first-generation and second-generation Camaros with the center port grille. But we made a conscious decision that we feel that we kind of own that cross-car slot graphic. Unlike the original 1970 1/2 Camaro with that center port aperture, there weren't a lot of cars that did that at the time—Jaguar and Ferrari. But currently there are a lot of vehicles that are doing that or a variation of the center port opening and we felt we wanted to stay the course and continue to develop strong cross-car apertures with its character that emphasizes the car's width.

At the same time, the team sought to take advantage of new lamp technology.

"It's still instantaneously recognizable and there are a lot of surprises with the level of [lighting] sophistication," Peters added.

In essence, earlier versions of the Camaro represent a tough act to follow. The older models still look good on the road because they offer a simple, powerful statement that has been executed beautifully.

The Sixth-Gen Camaro: What's Different

The new car provided an opportunity to upgrade the RS version and make it more distinguished from the SS or other trim levels.

The new light signature includes high-tech, low-profile headlamps with vertical daytime running and marker lights in the lower front fascia—except on the SS version, which gets larger front air vents for brake cooling.

At the rear, a new double-L trim wraps the side and bottom of the lamps for a new taillight signature, and the lamps have so much depth in themselves that they're three-dimensional.

December, 2012: Covers removed from the two final candidates to be the sixth-generation Chevrolet Camaro. *GM*

Team photo: Sixth-generation Chevrolet Camaro and its exterior design team. *GM*

Fine-tuning continues throughout the late winter and spring of 2013 on the final two candidates, including the convertible versions. *GM*

To enhance airflow through the nose of the SS, the lower grille mesh has a draft angle of 13 degrees, compared with 20 on the other versions.

"No one would ever notice if you put them side by side," said design engineering manager Mike Delor, "but it gave us 1 percent more airflow."

Peters said close work between design, engineering, and manufacturing was a huge enabler for the new car.

"Everybody understood what it takes to get this car right," he said.

The new Camaro spent some 350 hours in the GM wind tunnel and in a racing team's rolling-road tunnel in North Carolina to enhance its aerodynamic efficiency—minimizing drag and reducing lift while also meeting powertrain cooling requirements. A front air dam was replaced by front-tire deflectors to direct air where it was needed, while underbody panels reduced drag and joined new rear spoilers to reduce lift. Even the exterior rearview mirrors were tuned for less drag.

The roof cross-section was lowered, especially through the central section of what is known as a "reverse Mohawk," and the roofline of the coupe also benefited from the availability of laser-brazed welding, a technology formerly used on vehicles like Cadillacs.

Above: Tom Peters (in cap), Ken Parkinson (Executive Director of Chevrolet Design), and Rich Sheer (right) consider a full-size clay model. Details often differ on the two sides of the models. Note, for example, the different lower air intakes on the two sides of the lower front bumper. *GM*

Right: Hwasup Lee checks the details. *GM*

The car's rear quarter panels are muscular and the roof nestles between the rear fenders, much like the canopy on a jetfighter aircraft.

The goal, Lee said, was to "optimize every millimeter available."

Speaking of millimeters (which engineers and designers do, but we'll translate to inches here), the new Camaro is 2.3 inches shorter in length, 0.8 inches narrower, and 1.1 inches lower in overall height compared to the fifth-generation model. It also is around 200–300 pounds lighter.

After its unveiling in May 2015, one media report on the new car noted that, "If the fifth-gen Camaro was a burly Superman-type, the sixth-generation is more like the sinewy Spartans from the movie *300*."

Hwasup Lee loves that quote.

June, 2013: Another major review in the GM Design courtyard. *GM*

Early fall, 2013: Ed Welburn and Tom Peters with the sixth-generation Chevrolet Camaro SS full-size clay model. *GM*

Hwasup Lee, lead exterior designer for the sixth-generation Chevrolet Camaro. *GM*

CHAPTER FIVE
INTERIOR DESIGN

Above and following pages: GM designers submitted many ideas for the interior styling of the sixth-generation Chevrolet Camaro, and then continued to develop them during the months as the theme evolved. *GM*

"When I bring my brand new Camaro home and show it to my next-door neighbor, what am I going to brag about?" is one of the many questions Cheryl Pilcher asks in her role as the product planning manager for Chevrolet's two-door sports coupe.

Yes, there are such obvious things as the car's dynamic performance, how it sounds when it's not moving, the exhaust note of the various engines at start up and idle, and the proportions and details of its exterior styling. Owners of the new Camaro convertible will likely show off how they can lower the top from outside the car, with the touch of a button on the key fob.

The real source of bragging rights for Camaro owners, though, will be the features of the car's interior. After all, that's where those owners will spend the majority of their time with the car.

"The Camaro is all about having fun as a driver and the interior is designed around that," explained Ryan Vaughan, who became design manager for GM performance car interiors, including the sixth-generation Camaro, after being the lead interior designer on the seventh-generation Chevrolet Corvette.

"You have to make a bold move forward," he said of the generational change from the fifth-gen Camaro, introduced in 2010, to the sixth-generation car to be launched

Ryan Vaughan, Camaro interior design manager. *GM*

" 'WHEN I BRING MY BRAND-NEW CAMARO HOME AND SHOW IT TO MY NEXT-DOOR NEIGHBOR, WHAT AM I GOING TO BRAG ABOUT?' "

for the 2016 model year. "It's about creating a modern muscle car statement through powerful design, quality materials, and advanced technology."

Compartment

The newest Camaro was designed to establish a prominent entry point for the car. Its more muscular, bolder "form language" should greet driver and passenger alike from the moment they open the doors.

"So our challenge from the beginning was to do this in a way that is totally modern and completely new," Vaughan said, "but still inherently and intuitively feels like Camaro."

Another challenge was to enhance the sense of width in the passenger compartment, based as it is on the smaller Alpha platform. This was done in part by pushing the dashboard and extending the visual elements into the doors: open either door of the new Camaro and you see the bold new "boomerang graphic."

"The boomerang graphic on the doors is totally fresh and new. This was an idea from the early sketch phrase that was so distinctive, we knew we had to incorporate it into the final design," said Tristan Murphy, lead creative designer for the car's interior. "It still feels like a Camaro door, but now it includes this interesting sculptural shape that also incorporates the soft armrest, door bolster, and knee pads."

Instrument Panel and Dashboard

On the driver's side, the instrument panel design was inspired by the original Camaro.

"The first-generational Camaro has that IP that's just like this wall that comes up," Vaughan said:

It's almost parallel to the windshield and it's very dramatic. We couldn't really replicate that with today's vehicle standards for air bags and knee bolsters, but we re-interpreted it with a section that is just as distinctive, yet has a modern muscle car feel to it. The focus for the IP was the beginning of getting everything in the interior slim and low.

While the original Camaro had a virtually flat surface across the top of the dashboard, the sixth-generation features an instrument cluster bracketed by what almost looks like

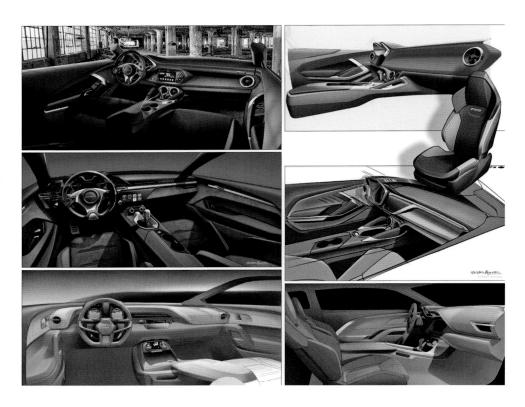

stan murphy 14

a pair of parentheses that curl above the panel to highlight the two large, round, primary mechanical gauges—tachometer on the left and speedometer on the right. Between these gauges, a display screen is molded from a two-shot lens process designed to eliminate unwanted light and glare.

"The cluster and big gauges are important, but everything else goes down and away from it to keep the visibility as open as possible," Vaughan said. "It's a more modern and less retro appearance."

It's also a case of "giving more than you expect in the segment," said Murphy, who noted that many performance cars offer less in technology despite being more expensive.

Many fifth-generation Camaros were ordered with a retro-style four-pack gauge set located at the forward edge of the center console. The information they provided in earlier versions can now be displayed on a reconfigurable screen between the speedometer and tach.

"The four-pack gauges were a retro cue in the fifth-gen car," Vaughan said. "They were really cool but not very functional. It was hard to read them while driving. With the technology we have in the new Camaro instrument cluster, we can display a lot more information clearly to the driver."

In fact, he said, the display within the gauge cluster adds "20 more sources of information" for the driver.

"It still has the cool factor," he said, "but it's also a real, functional driver's car."

Providing visual and functional impact is the car's new and smaller racing-style,

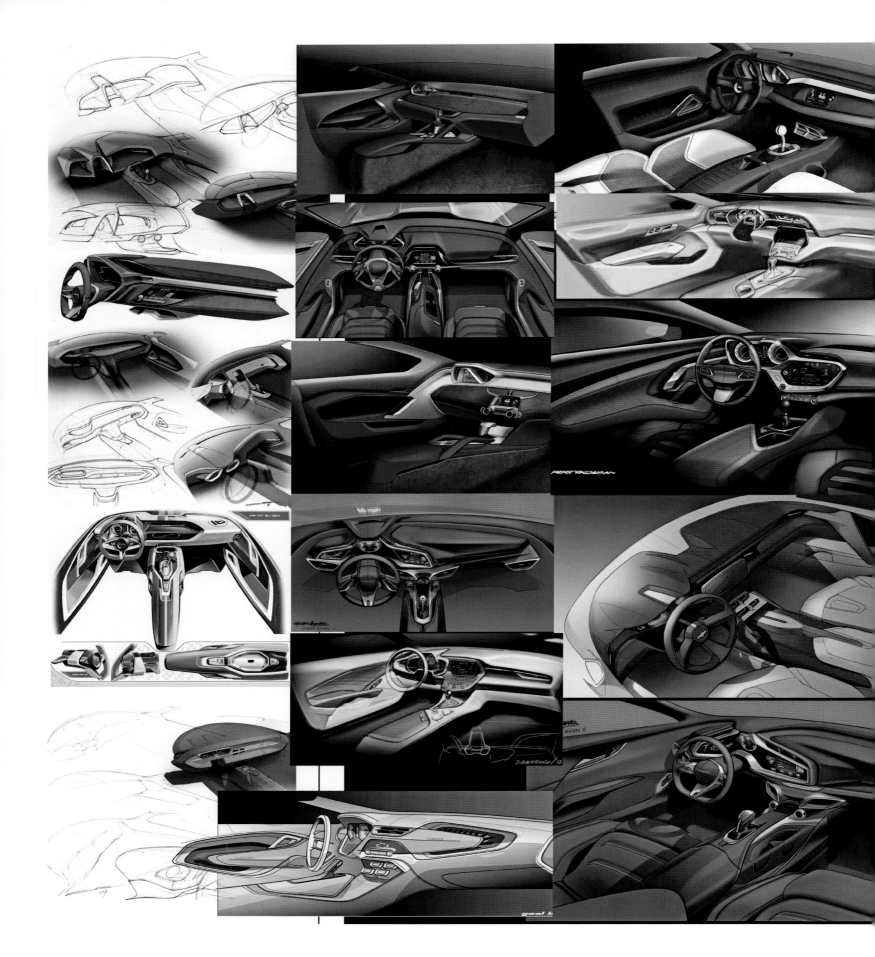

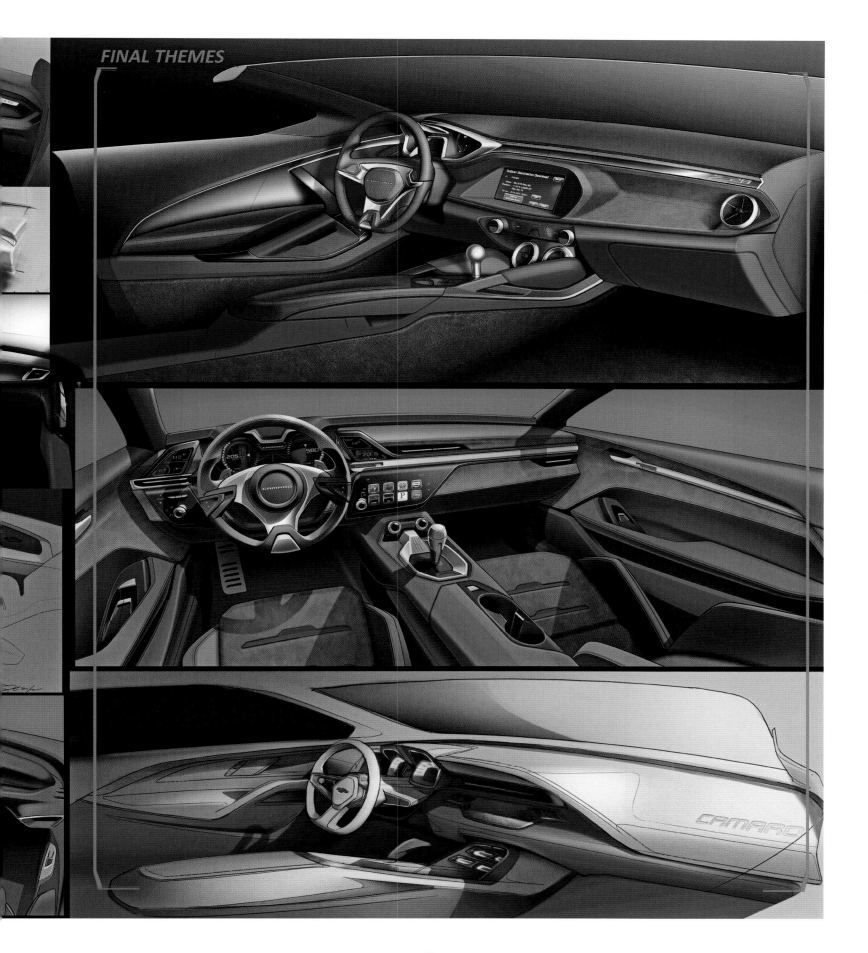

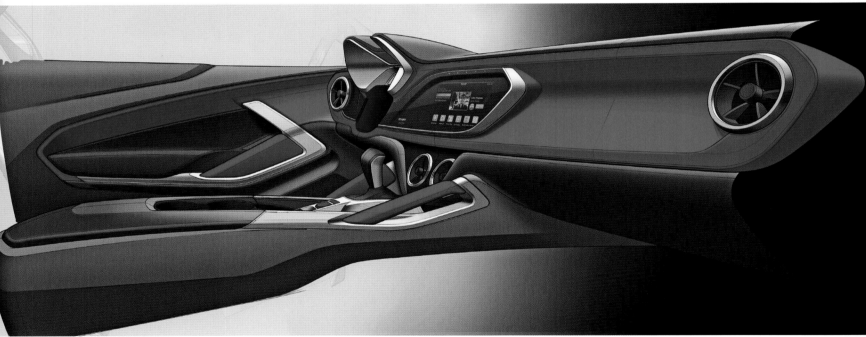

" 'YOU HAVE TO MAKE A BOLD MOVE FORWARD,' INTERIOR GM
DESIGNER RYAN VAUGHAN SAID, 'IT'S ABOUT CREATING A MODERN
MUSCLE CAR STATEMENT THROUGH POWERFUL DESIGN, QUALITY
MATERIALS, AND ADVANCED TECHNOLOGY.' "

flat-bottom steering wheel. The wheel is 360 millimeters in diameter, bears the new Camaro badge, and, for the first time, offers an optional heating system. That means it's warm to the touch for winter driving.

"We wanted something special for Camaro that was grown-up, mature, and it works," Vaughan said. "You can really use it and it really feels good."

The new steering wheel incorporates paddle-shift controls on Camaros with automatic transmissions, or the Active Rev-Matching switch on cars with manual gearboxes. The shifters also are new and, while the seat frames came with the Alpha platform, they have an all new design with a distinctive insert shape meant to evoke the low-back buckets from early Camaros. The bolsters are enhanced for added lateral support. They also offer optional heat and ventilation technology.

Push-button starter technology helps to clean up the dashboard by getting rid of the traditional key-turned starter. This also eliminates the need to have a key ring hanging off the dash.

Tristan Murphy, lead creative designer for the sixth-gen Camaro interior, shows Ryan Vaughan, interior design manager for GM performance cars, design details in a full-size clay model, or "buck." *GM*

Above and following pages: Just as with exterior design, full-size clay models are created so designers, engineers, and executives can experience a car's interior in full scale. *GM*

Central Console, Gear Shift, and Parking Brake

A major factor in the improved functionality of the car is its center console.

Even before any sketches were completed, the interior design team established a goal of improving the driver's access to the shifter by moving the cup holders out of the way.

In the fifth-generation car, "the cup holders are in line with the shifter, so your elbow ends up in them when you're shifting," Vaughan said. "It doesn't feel good, and when there is a cup there, it is even worse. We knew we wanted to get the cups off the centerline position and chose a theme that put more of a focus on the driving dynamic."

Eliminating the retro four-gauge cluster opened some real estate, and so did switching to an electronic parking brake, which eliminated the brake handle. The parking brake is operated by a simple switch on the console, which also provides room for the new driving mode selector.

"The enabler was the electronic parking brake," said Vaughan. "Without a mechanical brake mechanism we had the space to move the cup holders to the right- out of the way of the shifter- and extend the soft armrest forward on the driver's side, making it a lot more functional."

The console also was extended rearward to the rear seat, bridging a space that generally was unused. There is also a storage and a "cord-pass-thru" to keep cords for digital devices out of the way and out of sight. (The sixth-generation Camaro also offers an optional "inductive"—cordless—charging feature for smartphones.)

Another major step in making the most of the tighter dimensions of the Camaro's new Alpha architecture was the engineering of functional air-vent control rings, which allowed designers to position the two primary air vents much lower on the dashboard.

The trim rings around the vents are more than decorative: as the driver or passenger rotates them, they adjust the temperature and fan speed.

"ON THE DRIVER'S SIDE, THE INSTRUMENT PANEL WAS INSPIRED BY THE ORIGINAL CAMARO."

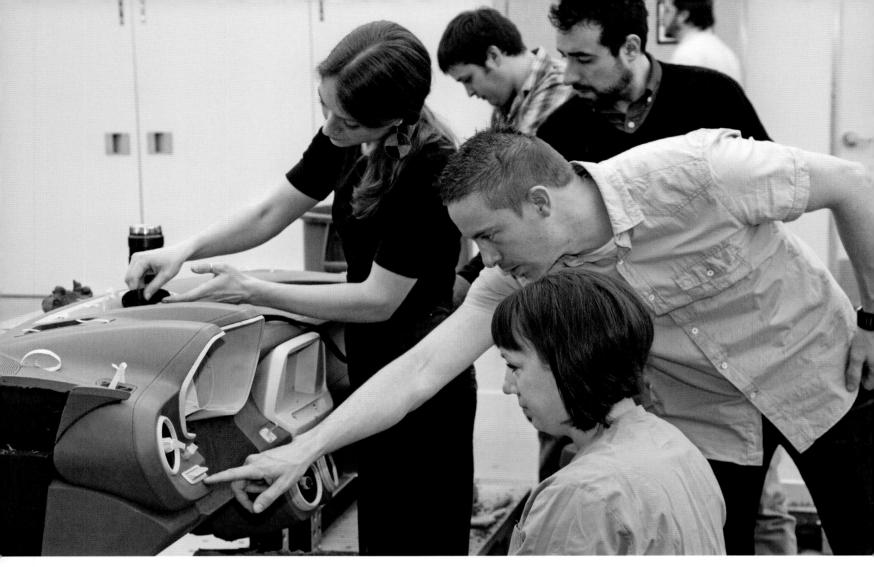

Illustration shows various lighting color options. *GM*

"We feel this is an innovative, clever concept that is distinctive within the industry," Murphy said. "Be relocating the vents down, it allowed us to keep the top of the dashboard low, improving outward visibility and sense of spaciousness." The dashboard houses a reconfigurable 8-inch display, which incorporates Chevrolet's MyLinkInk infotainment technology. Vaughan added that the screen contains a lens instead of a frame, providing "an integrated, high-tech appearance." The screen also displays another new Camaro feature: a back-up camera.

According to Pilcher, this feature addresses of the most common complaints about the fifth-generation Camaro: drivers had a hard time seeing what was behind the car.

Initially, this posed a challenge, since the primary reason people buy the car in the first place is its styling. When told that bringing down the beltline and making the rear C-pillars thinner would enhance rearward visibility, the overwhelming response was "Don't you dare!" Using technological solutions instead, the designers combined the back-up camera system in addition to a cross-traffic alert and blind-spot detection in the exterior rearview mirrors.

Narrower trim on the A-pillars, while enhancing outward visibility, also supports the roof and contains wiring for the side-curtain airbags.

Even the glove box was redesigned.

"We went with a different glove box door in order to maximize space and improve the feeling of openness in the cabin," noted Tim Wilde, interior program vehicle systems

Above: Illustration shows how HVAC controls would operate. *GM*

Opposite: Center console design study. *GM*

While the frame is shared, sixth-generation Chevrolet Camaro gets its own unique seat design. *GM*

> " 'THIS NEW LIGHTING SYSTEM SHOWCASES 24 DIFFERENT COLORS IN FOUR DIFFERENT MODES,' EXPLAINS NATHAN DRESSMAN. 'THE TECHNOLOGY CONTROLS EACH LED INDIVIDUALLY, ALLOWING FADE AND TRANSITION EFFECTS WHEN CHANGING COLORS THAT CREATE A SENSE OF MOVEMENT ACROSS THE VEHICLE.' "

engineer. "We saved a half-liter of volume utilizing a unique door with a special damper that provides quiet opening and closing efforts."

Materials and Lighting

In addition to updated design elements, part of the sixth-generation Camaro interior program included materials improvement. All major driver and passenger touch points received soft trim, with details that were cut and sew-wrapped rather than molded. Instead of painted metallic finish, aluminum or galvano metal was used for all metallic trim.

Perhaps the most brag-worthy feature of the sixth-generation Camaro interior, though, is the Spectrum lighting system.

"We wanted to do something different than expected," said Vaughan.

"We wanted to determine a way to get the Camaro lighting system to respond and react to the driver's inputs," said Nathan Dressman, part of the creative interior design team. "This new system will showcase 24 different colors in four different modes. The technology controls each LED individually, allowing fade and transition effects when changing colors that create a sense of movement across the vehicle," in effect flowing from the touchscreen outward toward the doors.

Working with the supplier Hella, the Camaro design and engineering team created four Spectrum modes: a lighting pulse that displays inside the car when the vehicle is unlocked; a movement of light across the vehicle at start-up; another such movement of

light when the driver switches to a different driving mode; and the Show Mode, which involves lighting "choreography."

"It's very theatrical. There is a lot of pop," said Dressman. But, he added, Show Mode is also "elegant and graceful [as] the light transitions and moves almost like a choreographed dance."

"We spent a lot of time working on how the light transitions as it sweeps across the interior," Murphy said. "It shouldn't be garish. It can't be Vegas."

Nevertheless, it's quite a show, so show mode can be displayed only when the car is parked.

"It would be too distracting while driving," Vaughan said of the Show Mode, which drew audible gasps the first time it was shown to potential buyers.

Tristan Murphy, Lead Creative Interior Design manager for the sixth-generation Chevrolet Camaro. *GM*

CHAPTER SIX

THE CONVERTIBLE TOP

The convertible roof of the sixth-generation Chevrolet Camaro features a hard tonneau that provides a smooth and refined look when the top is down. *GM*

National Public Radio talks about "driveway moments," when you pull into your driveway but, instead of shutting off the car and going inside the house, you sit and listen to the end of a compelling story on the radio.

Automobile manufacturers also like to provide what might be termed driveway moments, except theirs aren't related to something on the radio. Rather, they entail the car owner showing off the vehicle to friends, family, and neighbors.

The sixth-generation Chevrolet Camaro provides its owners with multiple "surprise and delight" features to show off in the driveway—and beyond. Among these are the two central air vents, with control switchgear built into the bezels, and the new Spectrum lighting system with its 24 colors shooting across the car's interior while parked in Show Mode.

There's another brag-about feature that comes only on the convertible version of the new Camaro: the convertible top itself.

Picture it: your new Camaro convertible is sitting in the driveway with the top up and your neighbor strolls over to see your new car. You reach into your pocket, pull out the key fob, press and button and— *voilà!*—the top powers itself down as if by magic.

And the top doesn't just go down: it disappears beneath a hard tonneau cover that emerges from behind the rear seats and closes over the lowered top, giving the car a neat and finished look. No windshield header latches to unlatch. No soft tonneau snaps to manipulate. No ugly stacked top blocking the rear view or interfering with the car's silhouette.

Such a feature is rare among automobiles. It's usually found only on exotic and expensive luxury sports cars. But there it is, on every new Chevrolet Camaro convertible.

"With many convertibles, you have to affix a tonneau cover manually—if it's done at all," said Tom Peters, director of design for General Motors high-performance vehicles. "The Camaro convertible's automatically deploying hard tonneau not only makes it easier to enjoy convertible driving when the inspiration hits, it ensures the car always looks its best."

And that's top down or top up. In the latter case, the coupe and the convertible share the same profile; the convertible top doesn't sit taller than the coupe's solid roof.

"The 2016 Camaro coupe will set the benchmark for the segment in terms of technology, performance, and design," said Todd Christensen, the car's marketing manager. "Adding the most sophisticated top in the segment brings another level of refinement—and driving enjoyment—to the Camaro convertible."

And that driving enjoyment doesn't suffer just because the top goes down, said Al Oppenheiser, chief engineer for the sixth-generation Chevrolet Camaro.

According to Oppenheiser, "From the beginning, the Camaro's architecture was developed to incorporate a convertible with uncompromised driving dynamics."

"With the convertible, we really wanted to up the game," he added, explaining that the convertible exhibits the same ride and handling dynamics as the enclosed coupe.

"Customers will appreciate what they *don't* feel: quivers, cowl shake, or an under-damped chassis typically found in a four-seat convertible."

It's not only in the driveway that Camaro convertible owners can show off their new car. The convertible top can be operated—put up or down—while the car is moving at speeds up to 30 miles per hour.

"It really does stand out above the competition for sure and above most of the other soft tops in the industry overall," said Betsy Philips, GM engineering group manager for roof systems, which includes convertibles as well as sunroofs.

Several styles of wheels are available as options on the new Camaro, coupe or convertible. *GM*

"THE SIXTH-GENERATION CHEVROLET CAMARO PROVIDES ITS OWNERS WITH MULTIPLE 'SURPRISE AND DELIGHT' FEATURES TO SHOW OFF IN THE DRIVEWAY—AND BEYOND."

The Best Convertible Technology

The order of magnitude of a convertible top development is pretty high. Adding all the features, GM spent a lot of time working toward this level of technology.

"From a GM perspective, we've struggled a lot with convertible top development over the years," Philips said.

> There are a lot of moving parts, and the generation 5 Camaro was a big challenge. But we made a lot of improvement with the next-gen [Gen 7] Corvette convertible and the sixth-gen Camaro was the evolution of our process. All the lessons learned from the previous years have been built into this top and the suppliers worked really hard to get the best quality product we've had.

That level of quality had to come without adding too much cost or weight to the car.

While a convertible top adds weight with electric motors and even structural support, "We've still kept the mass down," he added.

"In comparison to the Gen 5 Camaro, yes, it is a more expensive top. It's all power-activated. You trade a [simple release] handle [in the windshield header] for a[n electric] motor, and the articulating tonneau cover [and the motor that and mechanical components that operate it] probably is the biggest thing that drives cost," Philips said, adding that such a convertible top was part of the original product plan and thus the development costs were factored in.

The top can be put up or down while traveling at speeds of less than 30 miles per hour. *GM*

Beautiful with the top down, but the convertible top is just as stylish when up, and not only from the outside but in the fit, finish, and integration of the materials seen from within the cockpit as well. *GM*

"Knowing what we wanted out of the car from an appearance, from a performance, from a user interface, this is the way we want it. That hard tonneau is really the cleanest execution we can do and gives us the best interface with the customer and the best opportunity to maintain quality over the life of the vehicle. It was the right thing to do."

Though it wasn't easy.

"The [design and development] program did a wonderful job with the body structure team to be able to have enough space to fit the top," Philips said.

The weakest part [of a convertible top system] is the fabric, and if you don't have enough space to store it, you can have pinch points and other problems. Everyone worked with the studio to have a car that looked good but still gave us enough space.

It can be a huge challenge when you take the approach where we've had a car and decide to make a convertible out of it. The beauty of this convertible is that this car was always going to have a convertible. A lot of things needed for a convertible were planned ahead and we've been able to integrate that into the manufacturing process.

Another possible issue is actually installing the convertible top in the assembly plant. Philips noted that, to a degree, every Chevrolet Corvette is a convertible. Some are pure convertibles, and the others have a Targa-style removable roof panel, so they are all open-air cars.

While the Corvette assembly plant in Bowling Green, Kentucky, has long experience with such roof systems, the Camaro represented the first convertible ever built at Sainte-Thérèse, Quebec, then at Oshawa, Ontario, and now at the Lansing-Grand River plant.

"It's different than building a sedan or a coupe," Philips said, "but the manufacturing team has been very much engaged and supportive and they've worked with us hand in hand." According to him, the team is ready to build convertibles in the assembly line's regular flow while also completing them in volume and with quality—including control of wind noise and water sealing. This capacity for speed and quality is unmatched except, perhaps, in the luxury four-seat convertibles produced in Germany.

"One of the big things that people have trouble with on convertibles in general is the sealing," he explained. "Wind noise or water leak. Having a hard tonneau is just more robust. We really keep the water outside of the vehicle."

Philips said he and his team drew a lot of satisfaction from comments they received when the convertible was revealed, a few months after the coupe.

"One of the earliest comments I read was that 'Hey, GM finally got it right. They made a roof line of the convertible match the coupe.' That's a big win."

"I really do think customers will be surprised and Gen 5 Camaro owners will be very envious of those with Gen 6 cars," he said. "This convertible top is a generational leap. It really is truly better in every way."

> " 'THE 2016 CAMARO COUPE WILL SET THE BENCHMARK FOR THE SEGMENT IN TERMS OF TECHNOLOGY, PERFORMANCE, AND DESIGN,' NOTES TODD CHRISTENSEN, MARKETING MANAGER."

The convertible roof of a 2016 Chevrolet Camaro is tested as the car comes off the line at the Lansing Grand River assembly plant. The top is fully power-operated and can be raised or lowered while traveling at speeds as fast as 30 miles per hour. *GM*

CHAPTER SEVEN

POWERTRAIN

Empowering the 2016 Chevrolet Camaro are three engines
(from left): The LT1 6.2-liter V-8, the LGX 3.6-liter V-6 and the
LGT turbocharged 2.0-liter I4. *GM*

"One day I got called into my boss's office," said Al Oppenheiser, chief engineer on the sixth-generation Chevrolet Camaro. "He closed the door and introduced me to a couple of gentlemen."

They were from the GM Powertrain engineering. A veteran of the General Motors engineering and vehicle development program, Oppenheiser thought he knew pretty much everyone at Powertrain involved in the sort of high-performance cars he and his team produced.

But he didn't recognize these two men. Then it dawned on him.

"You're the four-cylinder guys!" he realized. "Let me out of here!"

With its turbocharged technology providing power and fuel economy, the Ecotec 2.0-liter four-cylinder engine could bring a new and younger ownership demographic to the 2016 Chevrolet Camaro. *GM*

The sixth-generation Camaro's new 3.6-liter V-6 was designed with power, fuel-efficiency and quiet operation in mind, but tip into the throttle and a wonderful sound emerges from the exhaust system. *GM*

Although Oppenheiser had been involved in discussions about equipping the next Camaro with a four-cylinder engine option to make the new, lighter, smaller version of the sporty coupe more practical for export markets, the immediate tone of the introductions in this meeting revealed that that such an engine was going to be more than a way to sell Camaros overseas: it would be part of the powertrain mix in North America as well.

You couldn't blame the chief engineer when his immediate thoughts went back to the early 1980s. At that time, in the name of fuel economy, GM's 90-horsepower "Iron Duke" four-banger had been installed in the Camaro and Pontiac Firebird for a couple of model years.

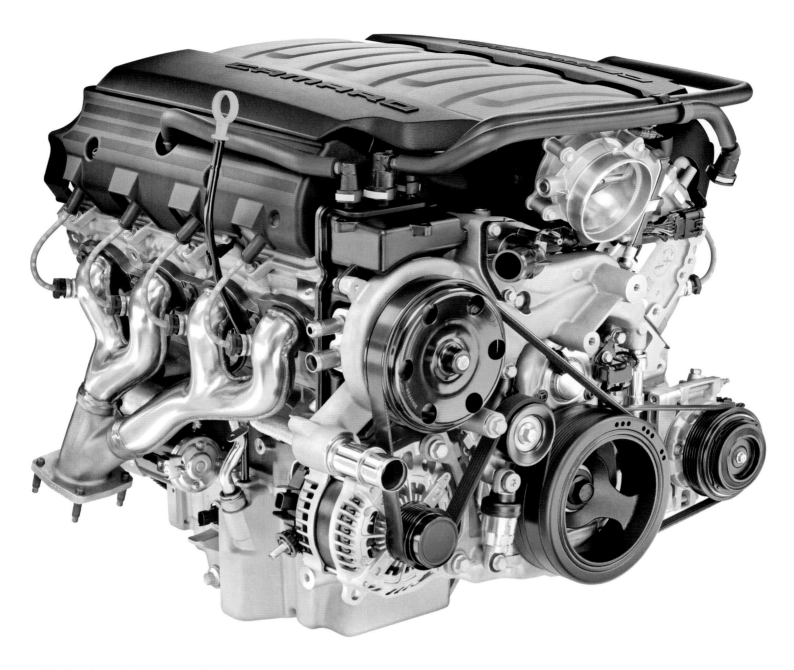

He also thought of the many hardcore Camaro enthusiasts who considered even a V-6 too much of a compromise for a modern muscle car. Now he was in a discussion about using an engine with two fewer cylinders in the latest and sportiest generation of the car.

Chevrolet's small-block V-8 engine has been a star since its original introduction in the 1950s. The latest version provides 455 horsepower to the sixth-generation 2016 Camaro. *GM*

New Markets for Four-Cylinders

Oppenheiser may have been skeptical, but he and the team were committed to keep the new Camaro development program from any sort of roadblock on its route to production. He was confident his team would find a way to optimize every powertrain option for potential Camaro owners. He also realized that a spunky four-cylinder engine could enhance the new Camaro's appeal, and not only in overseas markets.

The heart of the 2016 Chevrolet Camaro SS is its small-block V-8 engine, which provides horsepower as well as a powerful exhaust note. *Larry Edsall*

A new generation of potential customers was waiting right at home, younger buyers accustomed to and pleased with driving four-cylinder import sedans, coupes, and crossovers, and even some domestic-brand compacts. Powertrain's turbocharged four-cylinder engine just might attract such buyers to the Camaro.

In fact, at the same time, Ford was also laying plans to add a turbocharged four-cylinder engine to its next-generation Mustang. The Camaro's archrival on the road and track, and in the showroom, would sport a similar engine configuration, though the two companies took different paths in marketing their engines. At Ford, the V-6 remained the base engine, with the EcoBoost four offered as a more expensive, upfitted model between the V-6 and V-8 versions.

Four as a step up from six? If that seems confusing, you're not alone.

GM decided to follow a more logical progression. The turbocharged four would be the standard engine in the 1LT version of the new Camaro, with customers given the choice to outfit their vehicles with a full array of options. The V-6 would go into the LT2 model, while a small-block V-8 continued to power the Camaro SS.

Each engine would be specially tuned for the new Camaro, and each would provide its more-than-sufficient power to the Camaro's rear wheels through the latest generation of GM Powertrain's eight-speed automatic or six-speed manual transmissions.

"This is the best-integrated Camaro from a powertrain standpoint that we have ever built," said Bill Nichols, powertrain vehicle system engineer for the sixth-generation Camaro development team.

General Motors introduced its newest generation of four-cylinder engines for the 2013 model year. Large Ecotec (LE) is the family name for a group of powerplants that range from 2.0 to 2.5 liters of displacement. The architecture was designed for global use and enhanced refinement, reduced noise, and increased fuel economy.

One member of the LE family is a turbocharged 2.0-liter that provides amazing torque while running quietly and efficiently. For the 2016 model year, versions of that turbo 2.0 go into several GM products, including the Cadillac CT6, CTS, and ATS for the North American market, as well as the new sixth-generation Chevrolet Camaro.

In the Camaro, the engine is tuned to provide what has been V-6-like output—275 horsepower and 295 pound-feet of torque (which is, indeed, even more twisting power than is offered in the Chevrolet's latest V-6). Enhancing the engine's performance in the next-generation Camaro are a less-restrictive exhaust system (for more power and the sort of sound quality Camaro drivers expect from their cars), quicker shifts when linked to the eight-speed automatic transmission, and different gearing in the six-speed manual gearbox to provide for faster acceleration.

"It feels like a V-8 of old, maybe better," said Mike Katerberg, chief engineer for the Ecotec turbo four.

Mark Reuss, GM's executive vice president of global product development (and thus a kind of chief car officer), noted that the turbo four takes the new 1LT Camaro from a standing start to 60 miles per hour in just 5.4 seconds. As he pointed out, this is the same amount of time as the storied V-8-powered Chevrolet Chevelle SS 396 from the classic Detroit muscle car era.

LE Features

Katerberg said the new engine family development program started with improving combustion efficiency while also making the engines operate more quietly. Internally, it features dual cam phasing, balance shafts, a steel crankshaft, forged rods, and pistons designed for durability with cast-in cooling technology. The lower crankcase is structural and made from aluminum with iron inserts. There is a variable displacement oil pump

"THE TURBOCHARGED FOUR WOULD BE THE STANDARD ENGINE IN THE LT1 VERSION OF THE NEW CAMARO, WITH CUSTOMERS GIVEN THE CHOICE TO OUTFIT THEIR VEHICLES WITH A FULL ARRAY OF OPTIONS."

and fuel injectors (the engine family uses direct-injection technology) are isolated for noise control, while a chain drive provides enhanced durability, noise reduction, and better control of frictional forces.

A twin-scroll turbocharger is used to maximize exhaust gas efficiency and improve engine responsiveness. The turbine housing is stainless steel. The bearings are constantly oiled and, to enhance durability, they are silently water-cooled to ambient temperatures even after the engine stops running. Air-to-air auxiliary cooling is available.

The oiling system was designed not only to accommodate oil thickness in cold-weather starts but to handle lubrication in high-g dynamic situations.

"These are three technologies that really play together well: turbocharging, direct injection, and cam phasing," Katerberg said.

A major focus, he explained, was low-speed torque. Ninety percent of maximum torque—295 pound-feet or 400 Newton meters in metric measurement—is available from 2,100 rpm all the way to 5,300.

"The V-6 has higher horsepower numbers, but we're higher in torque and at a lower speed," he said proudly, adding that, "Our torque curves are very flat. It's the right match for the vehicle."

"With this lighter platform, we're not able to apply a four-cylinder turbo that provides a great response and very good efficiency as a 'no-excuses' entry-level powertrain for Camaro," said Nichols.

"This turbo model will be a good definition of a modern and efficient sports car, one that's not an animal that's going to be expensive to feed with tires, brakes, and fuel," added Aaron Link, lead development engineer for the sixth-generation Camaro. Link noted that the LT1 is tuned to "make it fast and furious."

The Powerful New V-6

With the turbo four being so good—both powerful and efficient—"the V-6 has to be more than just propulsion to our customers," said Nichols. "We have to exceed their expectations."

But exceeding the turbo four wasn't the primary focus of the GM Powertrain development effort that produced the all-new 3.6-liter V-6 for the 2016 Camaro. This new V-6 has to be powerful, of course, but development targets also included making it more fuel efficient than the V-6 engines produced by a long list of competitors (several of them playing at a much higher price point). In addition, it had to run quieter in normal operating conditions than even the new 3.7-liter V-6 from Infiniti, a luxury-car engine as well as the industry benchmark in the category, according to Ameer Haider, assistant chief engineer for GM's new LGX V-6.

Haider said the design and development objective was to create a new and premium engine using cutting-edge technology that offers class-leading fuel efficiency, quiet operation (reduced noise and vibration), and class-leading performance.

" 'THIS TURBO MODEL WILL BE A GOOD DEFINITION OF A MODERN AND EFFICIENT SPORTS CAR, ONE THAT'S NOT AN ANIMAL THAT'S GOING TO BE EXPENSIVE TO FEED WITH TIRES, BRAKES, AND FUEL,' ADDED AARON LINK, LEAD DEVELOPMENT ENGINEER."

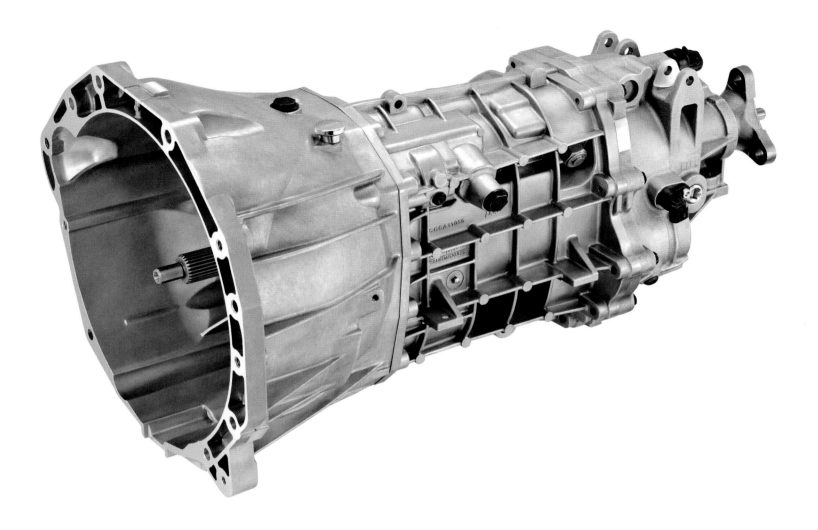

While it's a premium engine, the new V-6 from GM Powertrain had to operate on standard 87-octane fuel, not the premium unleaded demanded by some competitors' premium six-cylinder powerplants.

The Tremec TR3160 six-speed manual gearbox is available in the 2016 Chevrolet Camaro powered by an I4 or V-6 engine. *GM*

"It's a completely new engine from the ground up," Haider said, adding that this is the second generation since GM launched a "high-feature" V-6 engine family in 2003. Work on this latest version began in 2011.

To underscore just how new the engine is, Haider shared a small, bullet-sized lash adjuster assembly from the valvetrain and noted it was the single part carried over to the LGX from the LFX, which had been used in the standard V-6 engine for the last-generation Camaro.

"We have always been at the leading edge of performance and we're not going to give that up," Haider said, "but at the same time we wanted to make it the quietest and most efficient."

The new engine incorporates direct injection, variable valve timing and, for the first time at General Motors, active fuel management on a dual overhead cam engine. This

Headers for the sixth-gen Camaro V-8 incorporate a trio of Y intersections for optimized performance and fitment. *GM*

means that, under light loads, such as when cruising along an expressway, and when linked to the new eight-speed automatic transmission, the engine operates on four cylinders. The result is an engine that provides up to 9 percent better fuel economy, yet has the highest "specific" output among naturally aspirated six-cylinder engines, as certified by the Society of Automotive Engineers.

Haider said it also provides class-leading noise and vibration control and smooth, refined, linear acceleration. Horsepower is up by 12 compared to the LFX.

Chevrolet says the 2LT Camaro, with its 3.6-liter V-6 pumping out 335 horsepower and 284 pound-feet of torque, will reach 60 miles per hour in a mere (though stunning) 5.1 seconds.

Haider notes that hundreds of computerized simulations led to a new combustion architecture with compact chamber geometry, high-flow ports for a broad power band and low-speed torque, and an 11.5-to-1 compression ratio for high thermal efficiency. The combustion chamber design allows the engine to put out plenty of power, even in four-cylinder mode.

A newly designed intake cam phaser was added, allowing the intake cam to be retarded more than would be possible otherwise "without compromising cold-start-ability" and providing better fuel efficiency when driving. Also new are a single-lobe switching roller finger follower and a dual-feed hydraulic lash adjuster. The latter has two feed paths that maintain oil flow even when three of the cylinders are switched off; the cam turns but the valves remain shut.

Haider said new, GM-patented cooling technology is used within the engine. In conventional cooling systems, coolant typically flows front to rear and warms up along the way. The new targeted cooling system uses a parallel flow path so every cylinder gets coolant at the same temperature, allowing all cylinders to operate at a uniform temperature and "allows downsizing of the water pump, resulting in faster engine warm-up," enhancing efficiency and, especially, fuel economy.

New, too, are the valvetrain and timing drive with larger-diameter rubber-cushioned unround cam sprockets for reduced chain loads and quieter performance as the "non-round" sprocket shape cancels out vibrations. The chain also rides on rubber cushions to improve sound deadening.

"THE NEW ENGINE INCORPORATES DIRECT INJECTION, VARIABLE VALVE TIMING AND, FOR THE FIRST TIME AT GENERAL MOTORS, ACTIVE FUEL MANAGEMENT ON A DUAL OVERHEAD CAM ENGINE."

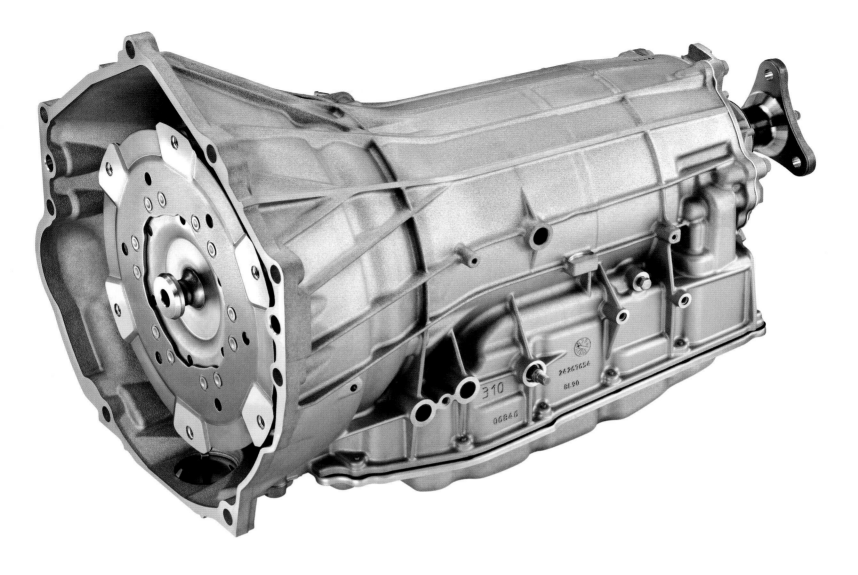

The LGX is also used in the 2016 model year on the Cadillac CT6, CTS, and ATS, though on those cars it comes with stop/start technology, shutting itself off at stoplights to conserve even more fuel.

"Typically," Haider said, "the Camaro customer is a performance enthusiast" who likes blipping the throttle while waiting for the light to change.

The new V-6, he said proudly, "bridges the gap between the four-cylinder and the V-8. It gives you the horsepower and acceleration and you also get the fuel advantages of a V-6 [or even more when it switches to its four-cylinder, 2.4-liter mode in AFM]."

Power and Fuel Efficiency in the Small-Block V-8

While the turbocharged four- and normally aspirated six-cylinder engines in the sixth-generation Camaro LT models may be plenty powerful and fuel efficient, those who want to get the most out of the car's lighter, more compact chassis will opt for the SS version, with its 6.2-liter Gen 5-LT1 small-block V-8.

As Jordan Lee, chief engineer for General Motors' small-block V-8 engine program put it, "The heart of the beast is pretty much the same as in the Corvette."

The 2016 Chevrolet Camaros with V-6 and turbocharged I4 engines can be equipped with an eight-speed automatic transmission originally designed for use on the 2015 Chevrolet Corvette Stingray and Z06 models. *GM*

However, accommodating the Gen 5 LT1 small-block V-8 to the Camaro's new Alpha platform architecture took some work on the part of both the Camaro engineering team and GM Powertrain.

"The LT1 is the heart and soul of the Chevrolet Performance car lineup," said Nichols.

"The LT1 is a great engine, with tons of torque and power," said Lee. "We wanted that same essence for the Camaro."

To get that kind of performance, the team had to change about 20 percent of the engine's components. For example, it required new exhaust manifolds.

"They're a lot different than on the Corvette," Lee said.

For the new Camaro applications and its narrower engine compartment, they created unique tri-Y exhaust manifold designs. These help the engine fit while also taking advantage of the small-block's cylinder firing order. Primary pipe pairs join cylinders 1 and 5, and then 3 and 7 on the left bank of the engine. On the right side, 2 and 4 are paired, as are 6 and 8. On each bank, those primary pairings collect into a secondary Y to provide the pulse separation of adjacent firing cylinders and improved scavenging for the engine's 1-8-7-2-6-5-4-3 firing order.

Benefits of this design include improved torque, with a modified torque curve featuring enhanced mid-range power, as well as better engine and exhaust sound.

Regarding power, the Camaro's engine is rated at 455 horsepower at 6,000 rpm and at 455 pound-feet of torque at 4,400 rpm, with at least 400 pound-feet available all the way from around 2,000 rpm to 6,000.

From a standing start, the new Camaro SS can reach 60 miles per hour in four seconds flat on a consistent basis, which means occasional runs in three-point-something.

And the car sounds as good as it goes.

"We worked a lot with Al Oppenheiser and his team on the sound at startup," Lee said. "The engine just barks on startup; it comes alive with a lot of presence. That bark is intoxicating. Exhaust valves in the muffler open for about 20 seconds at startup. I think it's the best startup exhaust sound we've ever had at GM."

V-8 Engine Design and Features

Engine features include an aluminum block and heads, steel crankshaft, piston squirters, direct injection, an 11.5-to-1 compression ratio, dual equal cam phasing, and active fuel

"FROM A STANDING START, THE NEW CAMARO SS CAN REACH 60 MILES PER HOUR IN FOUR SECONDS FLAT ON A CONSISTENT BASIS, WHICH MEANS OCCASIONAL RUNS IN THREE-POINT-SOMETHING."

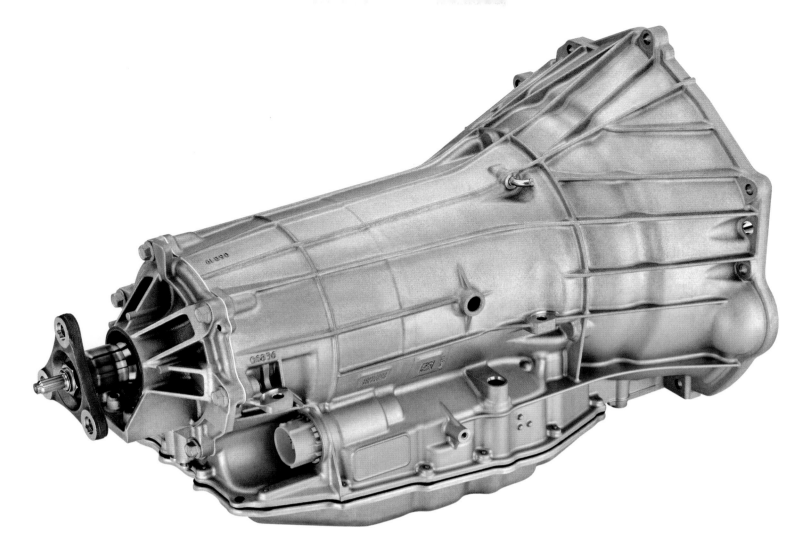

management—the V-8 can operate as a V-4 when paired with an eight-speed automatic gearbox—or active rev matching—when paired with a six-speed manual.

To make it truly track ready, a deep wet-sump oiling system was devised with 1.05-g capabilities.

While Chevrolet Corvettes received dry-sump oil lubrication systems for use on the racetrack, the Camaro's new platform didn't provide room for that equipment. By way of compensating, the coupe's added ground clearance provides for a large oil pan.

"We wanted a high-performance car accessible to the masses," Lee said. "We wanted to pull over 1 g in the corner.

"With a lot of work we were able to come up with a wet-sump system that gives pretty much dry-sump performance. It will do more than 1 g and will go around the track all day, and it's able to stay up with the tire technology."

As tires improve, cornering speeds increase, which means dynamic forces in turns—and in acceleration and braking—that are strong enough to force oil away from components that require lubrication.

"Oil sloshes to one side of the engine and gravity won't let it get back into the pan, but you can't starve the engine of oil," Lee said. "The large capacity of the new pan—10 quarts—helps with that."

The Tremec TR6060 six-speed transmission in the 2016 Chevrolet Camaro SS includes a Gear Absolute Position sensor that provides racing-style heel-toe shifting for smoother, faster shifts without years of on-track driving experience. *GM*

But there are situations where oil collects in the left or right rocker cover, he said, "and you don't want to burp that oil out" onto the racetrack or your garage floor.

> The other thing we did is really unique. We came up with these oil/air separators. Many cars have them, but they don't test to the extreme that we needed, so we devised a very interesting and sophisticated oil/air separator behind the water pump. Internal gases are vented through the separator. Oil drops back into the oil pan while gases go into the induction system to help keep it drier.
>
> It's pretty much a magic device. We worked on that one well over a year and a half. There was a lot of dyno work, and lot of track work.

Some of the work was done on GM Powertrain's tilt rig, a test dynamometer that can operate to nearly 1 g but uses only angles and gravity—it can't duplicate the centrifugal forces created on the racetrack.

The Camaro LT1 Lube and Vent System includes a valley cover separator and PCV valve in common with the Corvette, but also center-port fresh-air PCV fittings, the PCV Separator with drain to the oil pan, 10-quart oil pan with performance windage try, and pan-mounted oil cooler.

Other Camaro-specific changes to the small-block include packaging-related changes to the accessory drive.

A track-ready auxiliary engine oil cooler, auxiliary radiators, auxiliary transmission oil cooler, and differential oil cooler are standard on the SS. LT buyers can opt for a Track Performance option package that includes auxiliary engine oil cooler, auxiliary radiators, and auxiliary transmission cooler.

Transmission Options and Features

Each of the sixth-generation Camaro's four-, six-, or eight-cylinder engines all can be linked to GM Powertrain's newest automatic or manual transmissions.

The eight-speed automatic was created and launched for the 2015 model year on Corvette Stingray and Z06 and, later in the model year, on full-size GM trucks and sport utility vehicles carrying 6.2-liter V-8 engines. For 2016, it goes into the Camaro, some Cadillacs, and pickups with 5.3-liter V-8s.

"Our family strategy is to come up with a base transmission and tailor it on both ends to the specific vehicle application," said Bill Goodrich, assistant chief engineer for the automatic gearbox. The 8L90 for the Camaro SS and its new "little brother," the 8L45 for turbo-four and V-6, have been designed with the Camaro in mind.

"We keep as much common for economies of scale," Goodrich said.

So what changes?

For one thing, the 8L45 is smaller, with gears reduced about 15 millimeters in diameter to fit mass and packaging standards and to save as much as 30 pounds.

"With the two-family strategy, we can optimize for size and mass and performance for lower displacement engines, so small engines don't have to carry the extra mass," Goodrich explained.

The use of aluminum, and in some components even magnesium, makes the new eight-speed gearbox lighter than the six-speed transmissions even though it has two additional gears.

For another thing, the hardware connecting the gearbox to the engine and the chassis is different for different applications.

Goodrich said that nothing's carried over from the former six-speed automatic.

The transmissions have a four-gear set and five-clutch power flow architecture, with efficiency maximized by reducing the number of open clutches in any specific gear.

"The power flow allows only two open clutches in any one gear, which minimizes parasitic losses," he said. "We chose that for fuel economy and mass."

The chain-driven oil pump—an off-axis balanced vane pump—has two pumping chambers to improve efficiency. One chamber can be turned off when not needed—for example, at highway cruising speeds; this chamber was moved down to the valve body assembly in the pan and off the central axis. This results in a number of improvements, including about a 5 percent increase in fuel efficiency.

"Fuel economy is a fact of life. The customers expect it," Goodrich said. "But they also expect a good-performing transmission that can handle all of our new high-tech engines without compromise."

To take full advantage of new technologies and synergies, engine and transmission engineers are working much more closely together.

"We each have our own controllers and software, but there's a lot of synergy, shared signals and shared commands," Goodrich said. "The controller that we're using is processing hundreds of commands every 6½ milliseconds—that's 160 times per second—reading sensors, doing calculations, sending commands. And it's similar with the engine side, and part of that is that they're communicating with each other."

The new automatic also features quick and smooth shifts. "In some areas even quicker than DCT [dual-clutch transmissions]," Goodrich said.

When we were setting up our design goals, one was to be able to shift on par with the DCTs, because they are a large element for people who think the only way to get quick shifts is with a DCT.

The work that we've done to quicken shifts, we're seeing it on the track. The automatics beat the manuals in zero to 60 and in lap times. The algorithms are taking in all the sensors and g loads and anticipating driver needs to the point where we can shift more efficiently even than [a driver can] with the shift paddles.

Goodrich acknowledges, though, that "there's a certain customer base who wants to

"TO TAKE FULL ADVANTAGE OF NEW TECHNOLOGIES AND SYNERGIES, ENGINE AND TRANSMISSION ENGINEERS ARE WORKING MUCH MORE CLOSELY TOGETHER."

Powertrain engineers among those responsible for engines and transmissions for the sixth-generation Chevrolet Camaro include (from left to right): Jordan Lee, Bill Goodrich, Ameer Hader, Mike Katerberg, Todd Rooney, and Bill Nichols. *GM*

do it themselves. They enjoy the shifting. It's a great sense of control." He added: "They probably think they can beat the automatic."

For such drivers, there's the six-speed manual, again with one version for the SS and another for the turbo four and the normally aspirated six.

The Tremec TR6060 was used—with seven forward gears—in the Corvette, from which its Active Rev Matching technology will be carried over into the new Camaro. In the Camaro, the system is engaged with paddles on the steering wheel. Confirmation that the system is activated comes when the gear indicator on the center console's manual shift lever, which glows orange.

The patented system matches engine and transmission rpm, whether shifting up or down gears. An intelligent sensor known as the Gear Absolute Position (GAP) sensor anticipates the next intended gear selection event and matches engine and transmission speeds for peak performance by simulating the heel-toe shifting done by expert and experienced racing drivers.

"The GAP reads a [non-contact] magnet. When you shift through the gears, the rail rotates as it delivers the gears and the GAP sends [a signal] to the engine controller, then the engine adapts to the speed," said Todd Rooney, assistant chief engineer for the Camaro's six-speed manual transmission.

Active Rev Matching is the biggest manual transmission change for the new Camaro.

"The second most important feature is that we've transitioned from a single-mass flywheel to a dual mass with twin-disc clutch parts moving independently. This acts as a dampener, isolates and dampens vibrations, and produces noise and vibration refinement," he said, adding that, while the system adds mass, the tradeoff in refined performance won out in the end.

"We've also gone to a twin-disc clutch, 240mm each [instead of the single 290mm disc]. The small reduction in diameter makes a big difference in shifting, with lower effort and quicker shifts," Rooney explained.

For turbo four and normally aspirated V-6 engines, the Camaro gets the Tremec TR3160.

"The main reason is mass," Rooney said, noting that the 3160 is nine pounds lighter than the manual transmission used in the fifth-generation V-6 Camaro.

Rooney said that GM Powertrain also worked very closely with the Camaro development engineers. According to him, GM Design staffers even weighed in on details like shifter location and styling, to make sure it was "tweaked toward the driver."

Another area of attention was clutch-pedal feel and length of travel, he said.

"Not heavy or light," he said, but just right, and not only on feel but on the distance the pedal travels before the clutch engages.

Rooney notes that it "bothers me a little, to be honest," that the V-8 and V-6 Camaros are quicker to 60 miles per hour with the automatic transmissions, but notes that the turbo four has posted faster times with the manual."

But, he added, "volume penetration in Camaros is still very decent for manuals. The Camaro driver is one who appreciates the connected feeling that you get with a manual."

Oppenheiser Becomes Convinced

Among those drivers is Oppenheiser, whose skepticism about putting a four-cylinder turbo into the new Camaro evaporated on a rainy day in Germany in the summer of 2014. The Camaro development team was performing extreme track testing on Germany's famed Nürburgring racetrack, but one day rain washed out the on-track activities. Oppenheiser decided to take a turbo-four-equipped Camaro prototype through the German countryside, trying it out on everything from narrow winding roads through forests to the Autobahn, where he reached considerable speeds.

Instead of an obstacle to overcome, he realized that the spunky little engine was a hoot to drive.

"I had a blast," he recalled. "The car is lighter, the engine supports the quick-ratio steering, and it accelerates to 60 in 5.4 seconds. It rides the torque curve perfectly," he said.

He realized that the turbo four definitely enhances the new Camaro's appeal to the younger, tuner-oriented generation. And he sees another generation of buyers who might be attracted as well.

"There's no 'base' model anymore," Oppenheiser has discovered.

Each powertrain makes the Camaro an even more appealing vehicle to an expanding audience. That's the kind of problem every chief engineer would like to face.

CHAPTER EIGHT
GETTING THE CAR ON THE ROAD

Crazily patterned vinyl skins are used to disguise the design details of the sixth-generation Chevrolet Camaro during its testing and development. *GM*

When it came time to take the fifth-generation Chevrolet Camaro and turn it into a track-ready racer worthy of the legendary Z/28 badge, responsibility for the development program was put into the experienced hands of Mark Stielow, whose engineering career seems to have been a fast ride right from the start.

Even while studying in the University of Missouri's mechanical engineering program, Stielow worked as a General Motors intern providing support for racing teams competing in GM vehicles. After his graduation, as a full-time GM engineering employee Stielow took assignments that included turning the massive Chevrolet Caprice sedan into a capable police cruiser and pursuit vehicle.

Stielow left GM for a while. He served as chief engineer of product development at Summit Racing, then went to work as chief engineer at Gale Banks Engineering. Gale Banks was putting 1,800 horsepower beneath the hood of a Pontiac GTA, which won the title of the "world's fastest passenger car" by running 277 miles per hour on the Bonneville Salt Flats.

In 1999, Stielow returned to GM as ride-and-handling engineer at the company's Milford, Michigan, proving grounds. Soon, he was promoted to group manager for high-performance vehicle operations engineering.

That was just his day job, though. At home, in his two-car garage, he was building a new genre of customized American muscle cars. He even coined a name for them: "Pro Touring."

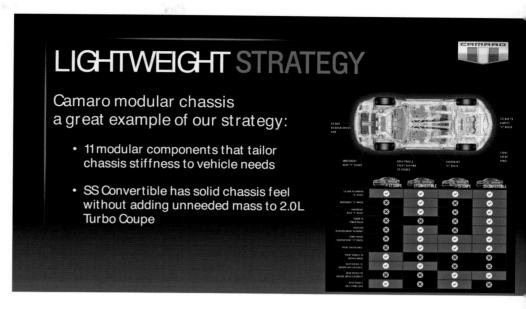

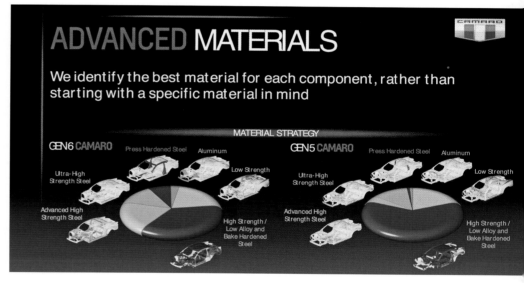

Top: Graphics shows how modular components help save weight without structural penalties on the sixth-generation Chevrolet Camaro. *GM*

Above: Graphic explores the use of materials and how they were specifically selected to make the sixth-generation lighter but stronger than its predecessor. *GM*

Stielow's Mule

Stielow's first Pro Touring build started with a 1969 Chevrolet Camaro and resulted in a car equipped with a 389-cubic-inch V-8 engine, which he twin-turbocharged to produce 1,021-horsepower (when drinking 100-octane racing fuel). He also produced a revised six-speed Dodge Viper transmission that could relay power to the rear of the car, where a revolutionary four-link rear suspension setup was in place to let the tires put down that power on the road.

"FOR THE SIXTH-GENERATION CAMARO LINED UP FOR 2016, THE MULE STARTED WITH A MODIFIED CADILLAC ATS SEDAN CHASSIS. THAT'S RIGHT: *THE* MULE. AS IN JUST ONE."

Not forgetting comfort, Stielow also installed air conditioning that would make the car comfortable to drive on cross-country excursions. A knob on the intake manifold allowed the driver to reduce the turbocharger boost, which meant the car could run on regular 87-octane pump fuel.

Popular Hot Rodding magazine covered the car's construction in 22 consecutive issues, and Stielow and Will Handzel wrote a book about the car entitled *Pro Touring: Engineered Performance*. When designers at General Motors started work on the revitalized, fifth-generation Camaro, they parked Stielow's car in the studio for inspiration.

Stielow named that first Pro Touring car "The Mule," after the early prototypes automotive engineers use in vehicle development programs. Even though they're cobbled together from existing components, such prototypes are meant to mimic the design and architecture of the next-generation vehicle.

When it came time to develop the fifth-generation Camaro, the previous version had been out of production for eight years; its F-body underpinnings were significantly outdated. For this reason, concept or show cars were built on Cadillac's smallest rear-wheel-drive platform, known as Sigma, and its mules were based on a version of the Zeta rear-wheel-drive platform used by GM's Australian arm, Holden.

For the sixth-generation Camaro for 2016, the mule started with a modified Cadillac ATS sedan chassis. That's right: *the* mule. As in just one.

"In the past, we'd have 20 to 25 mule vehicles," Stielow said. "In this case, we only built one."

When the fifth-generation Camaro was being developed, a couple dozen mules were constructed and used for preliminary testing. The idea was to use product planning, computer simulation, and vehicle math models to get the vehicle to 65 percent of its target goals, then to complete the development with prototype vehicles based as much as possible on parts created with production intent. Known as integration vehicle engineering releases (IVERs), they're used for dynamic development and testing as well as crash testing to verify they function as designed and can protect vehicle occupants in worst-case scenarios. IVERs are built on production-style tooling, with parts intended for use on the final assembly line—provided they pass all validation tests and prove themselves fit for duty.

It's not that the Camaro development team only wanted to build a single mule. The leaner, cleaner, greener new General Motors looks for ways to use math instead of metal; more computer-generated modeling and simulations, less old-fashioned, seat-of-the-pants testing and tuning, trial and tweak. Anyway, technically, these aren't mules but EDVs.

Based on these standards, the company expects to develop efficiently enough for the first IVERs to meet 80 percent of final target requirements.

Stielow's advanced vehicle dynamics engineering group works on pre-integration EDVs with "CA," the computer-assisted engineering staff, as well as development engineers with expertise in vehicle dynamics. The Alpha platform requires extensive modification to justify a Camaro badge. For this reason, only one mule was approved, for the sole purpose of testing the chassis and suspension on Milford's four-post testbed. This "torture chamber" is designed to verify that a vehicle's suspension geometry and kinematics meet targets even before the car rolls out onto the test track.

In addition to the four-post chamber at Milford, General Motors partners with Virginia Tech, a leading school in preparing automotive engineers and in transportation technology and product development. Together, they run an eight-post test bed located near Virginia International Raceway. This eight-post facility, known as "SoVa Motion" (short for Southern Virginia Vehicle Motion Labs), can simulate dynamic stresses like those subjected on 200-mph race cars.

Stielow's team took the Camaro EDV to southern Virginia and got the car running under its own power, allowing Camaro engineers to get some seat-of-the-pants experience while waiting for the first IVERs.

"It looked like a Cadillac, but it felt like a two-door sports car, except for its seating height," Oppenheiser said after driving the EDV.

The experience had convinced him—"We can do a great car"—and he knew the team could focus on tuning the IVERs rather than anticipating major changes.

Of course, even 80 percent was a long way from hitting the final target. There was still a lot of work to be done.

From EDV to IVER Testing

Aaron Link got his first crack at the Camaro EDV in February of 2013. As lead development engineer for the sixth-generation Camaro, he noted that the mule looked sort of like Cadillac's smallest four-door sedan, except for its much longer hood, flared fenders, and a "really wider track."

Like Oppenheiser, Link found the car to be "good from the get-go . . . really good out of the box."

But the car needed fine-tuning to ensure that it met GM's requirements and customer's expectations. Variant designs required testing. Three different engines, two different transmissions, and various wheel-and-tire combinations—all of these variables

Aaron Link was lead development engineer for the sixth-generation Chevrolet Camaro. *GM*

To verify early computer-aided engineering work, the Camaro engineering team was allowed one EDV—engineering development vehicle. Officially intended to run only on the four-post simulator test bed, the "mule," which put Camaro-intended parts beneath cobbled-together Cadillac bodywork, was nonetheless taken to the GM proving grounds test track for dynamic testing. *GM*

After being run around the test track in the summer of 2013, the Cadimaro (or is it Camillac?) EDV undergoes winter testing in Michigan's Upper Peninsula early in 2014. *GM*

Computers and wiring fill the trunk of and provide needed data about a sixth-generation Chevrolet Camaro IVER. *GM*

Above: It almost looks idyllic, the Goodyear test track overlooking the Mediterranean, but you can be sure there's nothing quiet and calm going on inside the car as it is pushed to the limits of adhesion on a wet surface. *GM*

Left: A blue Chevrolet Corvette Z06 joins the camouflaged Camaros at the Nürburgring garage. *GM*

Lower left: GM engineers closely inspect the car before and after its laps around the track. *GM*

Above: Chevrolet Camaro engineers examine the performance of the latest set of Goodyear tires on a wetted surface at the Mireval circuit. *GM*

"AT THIS POINT, IVERS ARE USED TO BRIDGE THAT GAP. THEY'RE TESTED FOR EVERYTHING FROM EXTREME-WEATHER AND CRASHWORTHINESS TO RUNNING THOUSANDS OF LAPS AROUND TRACKS AT THE COMPANY'S PROVING GROUNDS OR AT RACETRACKS, INCLUDING GERMANY'S FAMED NÜRBURGRING. IT'S IN THAT RHINELAND LOCALE WHERE ALL TRUE SPORTS CARS UNDERGO VALIDATION."

would be multiplied again with fixed-roof-coupe and retracting-top-convertible body structures and then tested.

The EDV, Link said, "was a great starting point. But where the team earns its money is in that last 10 percent."

At this point, IVERs are used to bridge that gap. They're tested for everything from extreme-weather and crashworthiness to running thousands of laps around tracks at the company's proving grounds or at racetracks, including Germany's famed Nürburgring. It's in that Rhineland locale where all true sports cars undergo validation.

Link and his team do most of their work on IVER vehicles built at Pre Production Operations, a sort of mini-assembly plant located just across the street from the historic GM Technical Center in Warren, Michigan.

Road trip: Engineers take the sixth-generation Chevrolet Camaro convertible prototypes on a real-world drive into northern Michigan in the fall of 2014. *GM*

A graduate of Virginia Tech's engineering program and a 15-year GM veteran, Link started at the company with a two-year introduction to all its operations and processes. This exposed him to a variety of engineering disciplines, though he said he learned quickly what he wanted to do, thanks to an early assignment shadowing the ride-and-handling engineer for the Chevrolet Corvette. With the orientation period over, Link became a technician for the ride-and-handling staff at Milford, a job that taught him a lot about all the measurements performed during a vehicle development program. Just as importantly, this job gave him a strong understanding of "what the numbers mean."

He applied that knowledge when he moved to the vehicle dynamics center and helped fine-tune the ride and handling of the full-size 2006 Cadillac DTS sedan. Later, he worked as a development engineer for the Cadillac XLR-V and CTS-V, and for the ZL1 version of the fifth-generation Camaro.

As IVERs evolve, the process can go through many iterations—but time is of the essence. The Lansing-Grand River assembly plant and various Camaro suppliers are all waiting for final validation, which gives them the go-ahead to create production tooling that will produce everything from body panels to bolts, from suspension links to tires.

Human Testing for Optimal Performance

While many items can be simulated by computer, others can only be tested by people working in actual vehicles.

For example, Link said, computer analysis indicated the need for a support brace linking the rear suspension cradle to the rear corner of the body's rocker section on each side of the car. What Link and his group determined, though, that cars subjected to the dynamic forces generated by the power of the Camaro's V-8 engine would need an even stronger brace. The solution—for SS coupes and convertibles—was to do a "closeout,"

Engineers hide the convertible top from any prying eyes. *GM*

Engineers and GM auto show staff turned a sixth-generation Chevrolet Camaro on its side to show structure and components otherwise not seen unless the car is on a lift. *Larry Edsall*

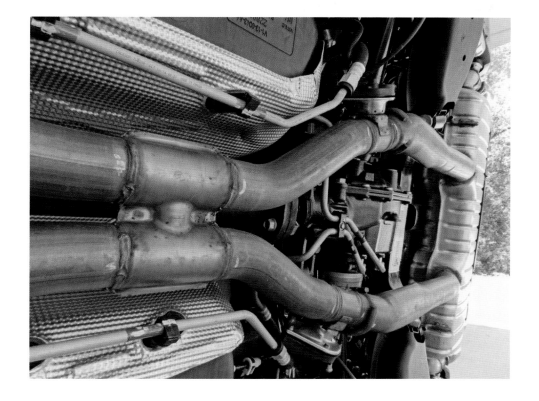

Just weeks before the start of production, Camaro engineers realized a change to the exhaust system would enhance the sixth-generation car's sound and the chief engineer approved the change because it was right for the car. *Larry Edsall*

enclosing about half of the brace's length with another piece of metal to create a fully boxed section. The result offered added strength with a nominal increase in mass.

Think of the basic brace as a section of gutter made from very strong metal: instead of the typical C-shape, though, the closeout section boxes in the open area, providing even more strength. While you can only see the change if you crawl under the car, Link said it was felt immediately when his team put the care through its paces on the test track.

"You'd never guess how much this transformed the car," Link said, adding that, in blind testing, "everyone knew it felt better."

And while there are limitations to what math alone can do, he said, such a change was possible only because the original math models were performed to such "high fidelity."

Human intervention is also needed for developing tires and optimized performance, whether in the quest for a smoother ride or a faster line through a corner. Goodyear earned the contract to supply tires for the sixth-generation of the car, which will feature extended mobility technology (EMT, a.k.a. "run-flat") for the first time for Camaro.

The Camaro LT will ride on an 18-inch Eagle Sport A/S 245mm all-season tire with an optional 20-inch Eagle F1 Asymmetric A/S EMT 245mm. SS models will get high-performance (summer) 20-inch Eagle F1 Asymmetric 2 EMT tires of staggered width—245mm on the front wheels and 275mm on the rear. While the wheels are wider than those on the fifth-generation Camaro, they also are six ounces lighter at each corner.

Each tire evolved through four full generations during IVER development, which saw improvements in road noise reduction and performance enhancements. By the end of

"EACH TIRE EVOLVED THROUGH FOUR FULL GENERATIONS DURING IVER DEVELOPMENT, WHICH SAW IMPROVEMENTS IN ROAD NOISE REDUCTION AND PERFORMANCE ENHANCEMENTS."

the process, the SS coupe was accelerating to 60 miles per hour in 4.0 seconds, covering a quarter mile from a standing start in 12.3 seconds with a top speed of 116 miles per hour, stopping from 60 in 117 feet, and pulling 0.97 g in maximum cornering.

"The biggest change is going to be the nimble feel of the car," Link said, adding:

This is a feeling that results from many changes, but mostly the size, the slightly shorter wheelbase, and the steering ratios that are quite a big quicker.

We drove an early test vehicle at the Milford Proving Ground on our autocross track and immediately noticed it really zipped through the cones. It will be a pretty big change in Camaro driving feel that everyone is going to notice. The more advanced driver is going to notice a better balance in the car, with minimal understeer. It's more of a natural feeling, one that expresses itself in the steering feedback and precision.

Each trim level will have a unique and customized steering effort, flexibility that wasn't present in the fifth-generation car.

"We have a very premium steering supplier [for this new Camaro]" said Adam Dean, vehicle performance engineering for ride and handling. "In the last five years, our learnings and abilities to tune components in Electric Power Steering have jumped dramatically, and customers will now get a state-of-the-art steering feel."

SS models get a fast 2.5-turns lock-to-lock setup. But the system will also be tolerant to things such as smooth road shake and road wander, Dean said: "The current Camaro is no slouch, but we looked to take the expectations of our enthusiasts and improve upon our outstanding balance during straight line acceleration and cornering."

It's a small reinforcement that fully boxes the Camaro's frame near the rocker panel and just ahead of the rear tires, but it makes a big difference in enhanced handling of the 2016 V-8-powered SS. The change was made during development testing and was deemed needed only on SS models with their higher dynamic capabilities. *Larry Edsall*

"EACH TRIM LEVEL WILL HAVE A UNIQUE AND CUSTOMIZED STEERING EFFORT, FLEXIBILITY THAT WASN'T PRESENT IN THE FIFTH-GENERATION CAR."

"There are some geometry changes we've made to make Camaro event better," said Link.

We took advantage of our dash-to-axle ratio and added more caster in the front suspension, yielding a higher tie-rod load gradient and more of a self-centering effect to the steering system. This helps create the steering valley feel we strive for and increases front camber gain with steer angle, which improves the front tire resistance to grip saturation, something that is a hallmark of many of the world's finest sports cars.

In effect, the front tire feels wider than it is, as though it had a wider contact patch.

"A larger strutrod diameter carries more of the bending lateral loads in the front suspension," said Holly Syriaque, Camaro chassis vehicle systems engineer, "and [it] lends you a tuning package that can isolate and provide better road connection for an improved steering response."

The engineering team's goal was to start where they left off with the fifth-generation Camaro 1LE.

Left and overleaf: The sixth-generation Chevrolet Camaro engineering team was back at Germany's Nürburgring racetrack in September, 2015, where an undisguised 2016 Camaro SS coupe equipped with racing seats and roll cage and other required safety equipment was pushed to see just how quickly it could lap the track where the world's supercars are validated. *GM*

"We love the 1LE and it's the sweetheart in our current lineup," said Adam Dean, vehicle performance engineering for ride and handling. He noted the car's price point and "incredibly good" track performance, which are further enhanced by its quality as a daily driver. But, he added, the development team's goal was to make the new SS model equal to the ultra-high performance offered by the previous version.

New Fixes, New Challenges

With each fix, of course, come new concerns. For example, improving tire performance with each new generation calls for tweaks to the suspension and dialing in the steering feel. Quieting tire noise can make other sounds apparent to drivers and passengers—and the way the car sounds was very important in fine-tuning the sixth-generation Camaro.

Link explained that the team spent a year—more time than is typical in a GM vehicle development program—to make sure the car's harmonics and exhaust sound character were right for the various versions of the new Camaro. Oppenheiser noted that all of those exhaust sounds are true exhaust sounds—real, not piped in.

That was important to the car's character, he said.

Early in 2015, Link and his team decided that, for sound quality, the single exhaust pipe on the turbo-4 engine should be split into two. Then, in mid-June 2015, they switched from an H pipe to an X pipe, just weeks before production was set to begin at Lansing-Grand River.

With the supplier already producing production parts, these changes might delay completion of the new vehicles.

According to Link, "Al's answer was, 'We'll find a way.'"

"WITH EACH FIX, OF COURSE, COME NEW CONCERNS."

THE ASSEMBLY PLANT

A sixth-generation Chevrolet Camaro body and passenger compartment and its powertrain and chassis are maneuvered into position for the "wedding ceremony" to take place at the Lansing Grand River assembly plant. *GM*

There's a big sign on the wall at General Motors' Lansing Grand River (LGR) vehicle assembly plant. Positioned just beyond the end of the assembly line, it proclaims: "Hearts, Hands and Heritage."

Lansing Grand River is newer than all but one of GM's assembly plants in North America. Even though construction on this site only began in 1999, its heritage reaches back to the dawn of the American automobile age. It was in Lansing, Michigan, that Ransom Eli Olds founded the Olds Motor Vehicle Company in 1897. Although his business partners later established a second manufacturing facility in Detroit (where Olds, not Henry Ford, built the first automotive moving assembly line), Lansing remained Olds' home. And it's where his REO Motor Car Company and the Oldsmobile Division of General Motors remained throughout Olds' life—and the lives of the car companies he founded.

Although a modern, flexible, state-of-the-art automotive assembly plant, Lansing Grand River was built on the foundations laid by Olds. The Oldsmobile headquarters building still sits at the corner of the new Lansing Grand River plant, which occupies a historic 111-acre site just south of downtown Lansing. This is where General Motors once built 88s, 98s, and Cutlasses, and where it produces the Cadillac CTS sedans and Cadillac ATS sedans and coupes today. Both of these Cadillac models are based on GM's Alpha automotive platform, which in modified form serves as the underpinning for the new, sixth-generation Chevrolet Camaro, also produced at Lansing Grand River.

In its original, 1960s model, the Camaro was built in assembly plants in Ohio and California. Assembly later shifted to Canada, first to Quebec and then to Ontario. The Camaro was out of production for eight model years until the all-new fifth-generation car was launched as a 2010 model. Then, in mid-December 2012, General Motors announced that at its launch, the sixth-generation model of Chevrolet Camaro would again be produced in the United States, at Lansing Grand River.

"Everybody was excited," said Mike Trevorrow, plant manager for both Lansing Grand River and Lansing Delta Township. An even newer assembly plant than the Grand River site, Lansing Delta Township was built in 2004 on a 320-acre greenfield site on the west side of Michigan's capital city. This plant produces crossover utility vehicles, including the Chevrolet Traverse, GMC Acadia, and Buick Enclave. It also has a metal-stamping plant that forms sheet metal body panels for other vehicles, including the new Camaro.

In a decision underscoring the company's commitment to central Michigan and its car-building heritage, however, GM announced in the summer of 2013 that it would spend $190 million to add a stamping plant at LGR as well. The new facility meant more jobs and also a projected annual savings of $14 million by producing body panels in the same location as vehicle assembly.

Adding the Camaro to the Lansing Grand River product mix also meant adding 500 jobs and a second work shift for that location.

Mike Trevorrow is plant manager of Lansing Grand River, where the sixth-generation Chevrolet Camaro is being produced. *GM*

"ALTHOUGH A MODERN, FLEXIBLE, STATE-OF-THE-ART AUTOMOTIVE ASSEMBLY PLANT, LANSING GRAND RIVER WAS BUILT ON THE FOUNDATIONS LAID BY OLDS."

Mike Green leads UAW Local 652, which includes the people who are building the sixth-generation Chevrolet Camaro, as well as the Cadillac ATS and CTS at the Lansing Grand River assembly plant. *GM*

" 'THE AMERICAN MUSCLE CAR COMES BACK HOME, TO LANSING, MICHIGAN,' " SAYS MIKE GREEN, PRESIDENT OF UNITED AUTO WORKERS LOCAL 652, " 'IT DOESN'T GET ANY BETTER THAN THAT!' "

"We have a great group of people building vehicles here in Lansing," said Trevorrow, a 30-year GM veteran who began his career with the company as a journeyman die maker.

"There's a long history here," he said, noting that many members of UAW Local 652 represent the third or even fourth generation of their family who have worked at the Lansing Grand River site.

"So the people are pretty good at it," he added.

Trevorrow said those working at LGR got excited a few years ago when they started producing the high-performance V Series Cadillacs:

And now we get to bring in the Camaro. It's an iconic sports car and we're getting a chance to build it back in the United States, and to bring it into Michigan and into Lansing.

A lot of responsibility comes with that, but a lot of excitement as well, to bring the muscle car back. We have a lot of Camaro customers who are employees and it makes them excited, and we've won over a lot of other employees who want to become customers.

According to Trevorrow, it's great adding the Chevrolet brand to the plant's product mix, "but having it be the Camaro charges them up."

In addition, Chevrolet and its Camaro will benefit from being at LGR.

"The Camaro is going to benefit from the Cadillac build experience, and from Cadillac-experienced builders," he said.

The attention to detail and to quality. We're building to the same expectations. Everything built here is to the best quality we can build to. And the building of some of the most powerful vehicles [the high-performance V Series Cadillacs] we have in the lineup also has brought in a little muscle car experience that we can put into the Camaro.

Building the Dream

"The American muscle car comes back home, to Lansing, Michigan; it doesn't get any better than that!" added Mike Green, president of United Auto Workers Local 652. "We're excited about it. It's putting a second shift back on. People are eager. I've not seen morale on the floor this high before."

And Green has been witness to much of that Lansing manufacturing history. His father and grandfather both worked at the Oldsmobile assembly plant. And two of his sons are working on the line now.

"It's a family business," Green said. "If it's not your relation, it's your neighbor who works here. And it's not just Lansing but people from a lot of small communities in the area."

Green, who hired into Oldsmobile in 1978 and is serving his third term as UAW Local president, noted that this won't be the first time Lansing has produced a high-performance vehicle. Even before the V Series Cadillacs, he said, there were the Hurst Oldsmobiles, a series of classic American muscle cars.

The sixth-generation Chevrolet Camaro bodywork is painted as a unit and emerges from the paint shop with its doors and hood and trunk lid all attached. *GM*

"Whenever you get a new product, everyone's excited," Green said, "and this car is part of American history."

And, when he thought about it, part of Green's personal history.

"I have not owned a Camaro, but I will now," he said. "My sister always drove Camaros and I always drove trucks."

Well, not quite always, as it turns out.

"Oh, I did have an '83 Camaro. Red with T tops. Crossfire fuel injection. Flaps on the hood that would go up and down. I burned a lot of gas just watching those flaps."

How could he have put such a car out of his mind?

"I got a lot of tickets," he said of a memory he'd suppressed for many years.

Like Trevorrow, Green said the Camaro will benefit from Lansing Grand River's experience building Cadillacs.

"When I came to work, it was 'you have three days to learn this or someone else standing in line outside will,'" Green said. "Now, the [extensive] upfront training is priceless. We were one of the first to go with that. You give people the tools and the knowledge to do their job and they won't let you down. That's been a big part of the successful launches here. The union and management believe it empowers people to do their jobs. It's the things that happen day in and day out that make your product successful."

"The Cadillac experience and attention to detail will only make the Camaro that much better," Trevorrow added.

He noted that Lansing Grand River management and UAW members were involved in the construction of the earliest of sixth-generation Camaro prototype vehicles at a shop near the GM Technical Center campus north of Detroit.

"We've had lots of good input to make sure this car will be built similarly to the way we do the Cadillacs," he said.

For example, because it builds Cadillacs, Lansing Grand River can use its expertise in laser-brazing technology to produce a more sculpted roof for the Camaro. This design will provide better structural rigidity while also eliminating "ditch-channel" seams and cover trim. It's an enhancement to the car's appearance that also saves more than a pound of weight compared to the traditional use of spot welding.

Saving weight was a big part of Camaro engineering's development effort. Connecting bolts were shortened to save a gram here or there, along with wiring harnesses, which over the years have grown in length and weight.

"Our folks have worked with engineering on how to optimize that," Trevorrow said. "We don't want extra, but at the same time we have to be able to build the cars effectively."

And it's not just engineering that has been involved in the assembly process.

"We've had the designers here," Trevorrow said, "to make sure that we're executing this car to what their vision was, from body-in-white through the builds, to make sure [that even] the paint is being reflected [off the car's body] the way they expected."

After all, he said, "We're building their dream."

"ADDING THE CAMARO TO ITS PRODUCT MIX ALSO MEANS THAT LANSING GRAND RIVER IS GETTING ITS FIRST EXPERIENCE WITH INSTALLING A CONVERTIBLE ROOF, WHICH CAN POWER ITSELF UP AND DOWN AT THE TOUCH OF A BUTTON."

The plant's attention to detail also means it's building the Camaro customer's dream.

"Camaro buyers like to customize their cars, and we're trying to enable as much of that in the [assembly] process," Trevorrow said, listing not only an expanded palette of colors but interior trim, seats, wheels, even various stripes being applied to body panels right at the assembly plant.

Adding the Camaro to its product mix also means that Lansing Grand River is getting its first experience with installing a convertible roof, which can power itself up and down at the touch of a button.

"It's a little different spin," Trevorrow said. "It's new to the plant, but we do it inside the plant." Although they take a little more work, the convertible tops are installed right on the general assembly line. "They travel down the line just like the coupes," Trevorrow said.

For those doing the work, this means both challenges and delight. "It's not the same vehicle over and over," Trevorrow said. "We're used to that with Cadillac. The Camaro does bring a different set of complexity, but we're accustomed to that here at Lansing Grand River."

To ease installation of the car's interior components and to protect doors during that process, the doors are removed and whisked away on a conveyor, to be reunited later down the line with their original bodywork. *GM*

Right: Doors off, work beings on installing various components. *GM*

Below: The famed Chevrolet bowtie emblems waiting installation on the sixth-generation Camaro. *GM*

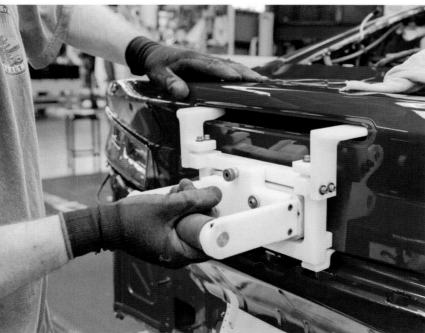

Above: A tool makes sure every bowtie emblem is placed precisely on the car's rear decklid. *GM*

Above: Immediately after being placed, the bowtie is checked and cleaned. *GM*

The Camaro will be the plant's volume car, quickly outnumbering the Cadillac vehicles with which it shares the assembly line. Trevorrow said the plant won't build cars in batches. "We've built our facilities to do flexible builds," he said. "That's much more challenging, but our operators are trained for that and it's not unique to Lansing. It's just the way we at General Motors have set up our facilities. It's a build-to-order facility."

Assembly and Installation

We can see what goes into making the new model great as we follow a new, sixth-generation Chevrolet Camaro through the Lansing Grand River assembly plant.

Lansing Grand River's own stamping plant is expected to go online sometime in 2016. Until then, sheet metal panels arrive from the Lansing Regional Stamping Plant at Lansing Delta Township. At Lansing Grand River's body shop, the panels are welded into a Camaro-shaped body-in-white. From there, they go to a Lansing Grand River paint shop that was updated to handle the additional colors offered on the sporty Chevrolet coupe and convertible.

From the paint shop, the body rides an aerial trestle and then down an elevator to the start of general assembly. There, it sits on a moving "skillet" as it makes its way along the trim line.

At this stage, the skillet rises from ground level so operators can remove the doors. These are placed on carriers that ride another trestle that carries them away, to be

Bowtie in place, the sixth-generation Chevrolet Camaro continues down the trim line. *GM*

reunited with the rest of the body later down the line. A parts trolley is placed on the skillet in front of the car and a couple of baskets carrying other parts are placed in the car's interior floorpan.

The skillet continues to raise or lower the car as needed to ease the installation of parts process, which starts with an interior wiring harness and seat belt anchors. Other components from the baskets and trolley are installed, including window trim and rubber trim around the door openings, and a pad is positioned over the transmission tunnel. Side-curtain airbags are installed, and, if part of the build, so is the sunroof.

The parts trolley is removed and the assembly line makes a wide U-turn, with a new parts trolley placed on the skillet. Hood latches are installed at one end of

Hand-guided power tools help lightened the load and enhance precise placement of the Camaro's pre-assembled dashboard. *GM*

The pallet automatically lowers or rises to the right height to reduce bending or stretching as parts are installed. *GM*

As with the instrument panel, tools help workers position heavy windshield and rear-window glass panels in the car. *GM*

the car while rear electronic components, including audio equipment, go into place beneath the floor of the trunk.

Various fasteners and brackets, along with the entire and pre-assembled instrument panel, are put in place. Throughout the skillet's movement, everything is scanned to verify that the right parts are going into and onto the right vehicle.

As the car continues along the line, another parts kit arrives. The headliner is installed, as are more electrical components, and then the carpeting—rear first and then front. Now the center console goes into place, as well as the interior trim along the sides of the rear seats.

Next to be installed are the windows. At this point, the bodies move from the skillet to a carrier, which lifts the body so that rear shocks, brake lines, and the gas tank can be added.

In another part of the plant—known as the chassis line—the car's powertrain has been assembled: engine and transmission, driveshaft and differential, and front and

Above: A new Camaro gets its new Camaro shield badge. *GM*

Right: About to be hidden from sight by carpet, headliner, seats and other components are an amazing array of electronic controls and wiring. *GM*

Not only the pallet but the entire assembly floor moves along the line. *GM*

rear suspension cradles, and exhaust system. This powertrain/suspension unit rides on an automatic guided vehicle that approaches from the assembly line's right. The powertrain/suspension trolley makes a 90-degree turn into an open spot on the line as the overhead carrier lowers the body to hover just above the powertrain trolley.

This is the so-called "marriage ceremony," with body and chassis braced and bolted together into a single unit. The components are now a car.

Above: The view from the catwalk above the assembly line. *GM*

Left: A section of the flooring carries a car and its pallet to another section of the assembly line. *GM*

The powertrain and chassis components such as brakes and suspension arms are assembled in another part of the Lansing Grand River facility and move on an automatic skillet toward their "marriage" to a Camaro body. *GM*

A sixth-generation Chevrolet Camaro body and interior move into position above its powertrain and chassis as they approach the "marriage ceremony." *GM*

Body and chassis are united in marriage. *GM*

Soon the vehicle can be driven. But first that car needs headlamps, front and rear fascia, and wheelwell liners, all of which are added on the "final" line.

Again, the line makes a wide U-turn, this time to the left. Seats are installed, then the car is lifted so that underbody panels and closers and belly pans can be added.

The car next glides into place between two spiral-shaped devices that deliver wheels mounted with tires, which are then bolted into place.

The steering wheel goes into the interior, the trunk is trimmed, and the car is lifted again into the air and maneuvered to yet another section of the line. Here, its various fluids are filled, the hood liner goes in place, and the doors reappear and are bolted back

Movin' on down the production line. *GM*

Spring and shock about to be compressed as body and chassis are united. *GM*

Lug nuts do their work to secure wheels and tires to the car. *GM*

A Cadillac follows a Camaro along the line in the Lansing Grand River assembly plant. *GM*

The steering wheel goes into place. *GM*

Bright lights help inspectors make final tweeks on the line. *GM*

A sixth-generation Chevrolet Camaro is ready for its final inspection and run through the in-plant test track and water chamber. *GM*

on. The Monroney window sticker is stuck and a large computerized monitor is plugged in for an electronic systems check.

This is where, for the first time, the engine is started. But the assembly process isn't quite finished.

The line makes yet another U-turn so that rocker panels can be fitted and detailed inspections can be made. Gaps are checked, such as the seams between the hood and fenders and the doors and quarter panels. Banks of very bright lights illuminate the car's exterior for close examination of surfaces, under whose glare the interior is checked.

Once everything is correct, the car is driven off the line and into a dynamic testing area, where it undergoes a hurricane-like shower to make sure there are no leaks. It then is driven over a cobblestone surface and through a tunnel with a specially designed rough-road surface to make sure there are no squeaks and rattles.

Finally, it goes past that "Hearts, Hands & Heritage" sign and outside to a parking lot. There it awaits its turn to be driven onto a car-hauling trailer for delivery to a Chevrolet dealership. From there, it eventually arrives at its owner's driveway or garage.

At the end of the line, the cars are driven into a water chamber to verify there are no leaks, and then onto the in-plant rough-road dynamic test area before final approval and being parked outside awaiting their trip on transport trucks to a Chevrolet dealership. *GM*

Sixth-generation Chevrolet Camaros are built on the same assembly line and undergo the same inspections and testing as the coupes. *GM*

Chevrolet employees are introduced to the sixth-generation
Chevrolet Camaro during a special event on Detroit's Belle Isle. *GM*

The sixth-generation of the Chevrolet Camaro is unveiled at a special event held on Detroit Belle Isle for the automotive media and Camaro enthusiasts. *GM*

NASCAR racer Danica Patrick and Camaro chief engineer Al Oppenheiser surprise Alican "Turk" Boyacioglu and his wife, Michelle, of Wichita, Kansas, at the Texas Motor Speedway in the fall of 2015. The Boyacioglus thought they were going to meet Patrick and Oppenheiser, and they did when they were handed the keys to their new car, the first 2016 Camaro delivered to a customer. *GM*

The fifth-generation Chevrolet Camaro's introduction was one of the loudest launches ever into the automotive marketplace: a starring role in the *Transformers* movie franchise. Longtime Camaro owners got an early look at the car's styling, but the film also showcased the Camaro for a new generation of future drivers.

"We have no *Transformers* to introduce this car," said Todd Christensen, marketing manager for the sixth-generation Camaro. "But the good news is that all the work we've been doing for the last five years has built up a lot of momentum. We're starting from a strong position."

Instead of unveiling the next Camaro in the traditional auto show environment, or through a big-screen blockbuster, the sixth-generation car made its debut in May 16, 2015, at a huge celebration on Belle Isle Park. This large island playground sits in the Detroit River just upriver from downtown, across the waterway from Windsor, Ontario, Canada.

"We have so many Chevrolet vehicle launches this year—five major models to roll out—that there weren't enough auto shows to do a [Camaro] reveal," Christensen said. "Camaro [already] has a lot of existing excitement around it, and a fan base, so we thought, 'Let's bring in the customers and let them enjoy the car.'"

"We're lucky. Like Corvette, we have a huge fan base," added Christensen, who was advertising manager for the seventh-generation Chevrolet sports car before moving to the Camaro team, "and you don't often get a change to bring your owners in to be part of a reveal like this."

For that reveal, Chevrolet brought out the new Camaro coupe and invited owners of earlier cars to bring theirs as well.

"THE SIXTH-GENERATION CAR MADE ITS DEBUT IN MAY 16, 2015, AT A HUGE CELEBRATION ON BELLE ISLE PARK."

The sixth-generation Chevrolet Camaro has its coming-out party and is displayed in various versions (except for the convertible) on Belle Isle. *GM*

Camaro owners were invited to attend a special unveiling of the sixth-generation car on the racetrack at Detroit's Belle Isle. *GM*

Above: A bridge leads Camaro owners to Belle Isle for the unveiling of the newest version. *GM*

Left: Camaro design director Tom Peters brought his own classic Camaro, a COPO-inspired 1969 ZL1 big-block coupe, to the unveiling on Belle Isle. *GM*

Owners of classic Camaros line the racetrack at Belle Isle. *GM*

The famous Roger Penske/Mark Donohue Trans-Am racer was among those invited to take part in a Camaro hall of fame display on Belle Isle. *GM*

"We had about a thousand people and our car count was somewhere close to 350," Christensen said.

Present that day was the very first Camaro, one of the 49 "pilot-assembly" cars built at Norwood, Ohio. The car, with an inline six-cylinder engine and three-speed manual transmission, bears VIN 1000001. It was used at the public introduction of the new model in August 1966, in public relations photos and promotional films; in time the car went to a Chevrolet dealership in Oklahoma. Sold and souped up for drag racing, it was raced before being restored to its original factory condition.

This car headed up a stunning lineup of heritage vehicles, including a 1967 Z/28 (one of only 602 built); the legendary 1967 "Grumpy's Toy" Super Stock drag racing Camaro; a 1968 Z/28 convertible (the only one, specially built for Chevrolet General Manager Pete Estes); a 1969 Camaro COPO ZL1 (one of only 69 such cars built with big-block 427 V-8 engines); a 1969 Yenko Camaro; the Penske Racing-prepared, Mark Donohue-driven and Sunoco-sponsored Z/28 Trans-Am race car; and many more rarities. The fifth-generation Z/28 was a standout that day, memorable as the car that drew 1.5 million YouTube views for footage of its storming circuits around Germany's famed Nürburgring racetrack.

Camouflaged Camaros used for testing by the engineers were on site at Belle Isle. *GM*

The site of this muscle car pageant, Belle Isle is home to several recreational areas as well as the site of the annual Detroit Grand Prix auto races.

Christensen is a longtime Camaro enthusiast—his father restored and judged them at car shows, and Christensen's first car was a 1969 Camaro that he restored with his father.

"We filled the racing paddock completely with Camaros, including 25 of the most significant historical Camaros, all in one place," Christensen said. "Some were from the GM Heritage Center and the others were privately owned."

"A secondary benefit was the media got to see the unveil as well," added Christensen, a long-time Camaro enthusiast; his father restored and judged at car shows and Christensen's first car was a 1969 Camaro that he restored with his father.

"There are pros and cons," Christensen said of the various ways to unveil a vehicle. "When you go to an auto show, there's more media there, but there are also confinements. [On Belle Isle] We had the ability to create our own schedule, our own venue, and do our own show."

This "show" included driving laps around the grand prix track in the new car. The day went well, except for some damage incurred by one of the new Camaros when a member of the media banged into a barrier.

About a month after Belle Isle, Chevrolet unveiled the new Camaro convertible at a special media event, also held in Detroit. Here, the company showed off all five of the new Chevrolet vehicles for the international media.

"The location again was here in Detroit, and that played to our advantage," Christensen said, adding that one challenge is to keep interest "churning" in the time between a vehicle's introduction and its availability in dealership showrooms.

Immediately after the convertible unveiling in Detroit, chief engineer Al Oppenheiser headed for England, where the Camaro coupe was inttroduced to a European audience at the Goodwood Festival of Speed.

A smartphone app with a function to spec out cars and see it in various colors and with various accessories was just one of the web-based marketing campaigns Chevrolet used for the new car's rollout. It was also featured at other national venues, including the annual vintage sports car races on California's Monterey Peninsula in

The sixth-generation Chevrolet Camaro was unveiled to a European audience at the Goodwood Festival of Speed. *GM*

NASCAR racer Kevin Harvick showed off his 1969 Chevrolet Camaro next to a sixth-generation convertible at the Woodward Dream Cruise in August, 2015. *GM*

"ABOUT A MONTH AFTER BELLE ISLE, CHEVROLET UNVEILED THE NEW CAMARO CONVERTIBLE AT A SPECIAL MEDIA EVENT, ALSO HELD IN DETROIT. HERE, THE COMPANY SHOWED OFF ALL FIVE OF THE NEW CHEVROLET VEHICLES FOR THE INTERNATIONAL MEDIA."

Shown at SEMA: The SS Red Accent package on a 2016 Chevrolet Camaro convertible. *GM*

Shown at SEMA: The 2016 Chevrolet Camaro Performance concept coupe. *GM*

mid-August. Eight sixth-generation Camaros, with customizations from GM Design ranging from mild to wild, were designed for the annual SEMA Show, the Specialty Equipment Market Association's early November gathering in Las Vegas.

When Camaro designers, engineers, and even marketing execs attend Camaro club events and national shows (many are enthusiasts, too), they often notice that the only truly "stock" cars present are the ones they've brought from Chevrolet's own fleet. It seems that every private Camaro owner almost immediately starts customizing and personalizing his or her car to make it unique, to make it their own.

With this in mind, Chevrolet has been more active in offering high-performance versions of the car in addition to a long line of customizing accessories. The sixth-generation Camaro makes many of these accessories available at Chevrolet dealerships right along with the first delivery of the cars themselves.

Gen 6 Concepts and Accessories

To show sixth-gen Camaro owners some of the vehicle's possibilities, Chevrolet's 2015 SEMA stand included:

- The Camaro Performance concept: a Summit White SS coupe, with new red accents (including an engine cover), billet-cut, 20-inch forged aluminum wheels, lower suspension, and Brembo brake upgrade
- The Hyper concept: a Hyper Blue, V-6-powered LT coupe, featuring white rally stripes, heritage-style fender badges, and 20-inch forged aluminum wheels

- The Black coupe concept: a blacked-out SS with Mosaic Black Metallic exterior paint and darkened trim, tinted glass, and 20-inch black wheels, its sinister look enhanced by lowered suspension
- The Black Accent SS coupe concept: an SS coupe with black ground effects, darkened taillamps, satin black rally stripes, black 20-inch five-split spoke low-gloss black wheels, and a black fuel door cover
- The Red Line Series V-6 coupe concept: a V-6 coupe featuring enhanced Silver Ice Metallic paint with custom fender hash marks, Satin Graphite accents, 20-inch wheels with painted Performance Red accents, mirror caps, grille surround and accents, and Jet Black leather interior with Satin Graphite interior trim
- The Red Accent SS convertible concept: an SS convertible with Switchblade Silver Metallic paint accented with red trim and Adrenaline Red leather interior, red inserts on the lower grille, red "hash mark" finder graphics, five-spoke gloss black wheels with red outline stripe, and a red-accented engine cover
- The Krypton concept: a vehicle featuring five-layer electroluminescent Krypton Green paint with Chevrolet bowtie emblems cascading down the front fender sides and glowing when the driver touches a switch illuminating current to the images

Also on display at the show were accessories that were available immediately with the car's launch:

- Three aluminum wheel designs in multiple finishes
- Grille kits with six body-color inserts, as well as a primed, ready-to-paint version
- A blade-style rear spoiler and ground effects kit (available in 10 colors)

"CHEVROLET SAID IT PLANS TO BUILD 69 COPO CAMAROS FOR 2016, AVAILABLE WITH EITHER LS-BASED 427 CID OR LT1-BASED 6.2-LITER ENGINES."

Shown at SEMA: The 2016 Chevrolet Camaro SS Black Accent coupe. *GM*

Shown at SEMA: The 2016 Hyper Blue coupe concept. *Larry Edsall*

Shown at SEMA: The 2016 Chevrolet Performance COPO Camaro Courtney Force concept car. *Larry Edsall*

- Four exterior graphic packages—rally stripe, front-fender hash mark, racing stripe, and body-side spear—each available in multiple colors
- Interior trim kits, again in multiple colors
- V-8 and V-6 performance exhaust kits with factory warranty
- Performance air intake for the SS
- Lowering suspension kits, including higher-rate front and rear coil springs, and specifically tuned struts and shocks that lower the vehicle 0.8 inch (20mm), with four versions tuned for V-8 or V-6 coupes and convertibles
- Brembo performance front brake packages that include 13.6-inch vented and slotted Duralife rotors, performance brake pads, and four-piston aluminum calipers in red for V-6 and Turbo cars
- Performance air intake kit for the SS
- Engine covers in red, blue, or black

More was on display in the form of the Chevrolet Performance COPO Camaro Courtney Force concept car. This vehicle, created in conjunction with NHRA Funny Car driver Courtney Force, will be auctioned in January 2016 at the Barrett-Jackson Collector Car Auction in Scottsdale, Arizona, with proceeds to benefit United Way. The COPO car has a 350-cubic-inch supercharged LSX-based engine, 3-speed automatic gearbox, adjustable front struts, adjustable coil-over rear shocks, panhard bar and anti-roll bar, 35-spline spool and rear axles, manual lightweight brake rotors and calipers, integrated line lock, manual rack-and-pinion steering, fuel cell with high-pressure pump, racing wire harness, NHRA-certified roll cage, racing bucket seats, five-point safety harnesses for driver and passenger, special exterior graphics, high-ride carbon-fiber hood, one-off rear spoiler, smoke-finished Weld drag-racing wheels, Goodyear Eagle drag-racing tires, plus wheelie bars and a drag parachute.

Chevrolet said it plans to build 69 COPO Camaros for 2016, available with either LS-based 427 cid or LT1-based 6.2-liter engines. And at the Chicago Auto Show in early 2016, Chevrolet unveiled a 2017 version of the new Camaro, the 1LE performance package designed for track-day use. In addition to a 1LE package for the Camaro SS, Chevrolet revealed a 1LE package for Camaros with V-6 engines featuring enhanced suspension, Brembo brakes, and Goodyear Eagle F1 tires for more cornering grip. All 1LE cars also get a satin-black hood and special wheels.

The 1LE package for the SS includes magnetic ride control, new FE4 suspension tuning, segment-exclusive electronic limited slip differential, Recaro seats, and a Performance Data Recorder (the seats and PDR are available as well to those opting for the V-6 1LE package).

Driven to Be 2016 Car of the Year

Even before the start of the 2015 SEMA Show, the Gen 6 Camaro was touring all 48 contiguous United States. Chevrolet's strategy was to give the automotive media a first look while also offering prolonged drives in the cars. The media tour event was held in

The 2017 1LE Camaro V-6 (right) and the SS version (left). *GM*

conjunction with Camaro club gatherings in sixteen cities around the country.

The tour ended at the Los Angeles Auto Show. As a preview of their arrival, *Motor Trend* gave the Camaro marketing team a boost by selecting the Camaro as its 2016 Car of the Year. The car beat out the competition in a packed field, which included the Audi TT, BMW 7 Series, Mercedes-Benz GT S, Toyota Mirai, and Mazda MX-5 Miata.

"Based on General Motor's stellar Alpha platform architecture, the completely redesigned sixth-generation Camaro is sharper looking inside and out and has the latest in technology, including Apple CarPlay and 4G LTE Wi-Fi," the magazine said in its announcement.

Shown at SEMA: The 2016 Chevrolet Camaro Krypton concept car. *GM*

"It's a car built for driving enthusiasts, one that is hundreds of pounds lighter than the previous generation and available with a new, high-tech, turbocharged 275-horsepower four-cylinder engine, a sporty, yet fuel-efficient 335-horsepower V-6, or a blistering 455-horsepower V-8."

"Our 2016 Car of the Year, the Chevrolet Camaro, is one of the finest driving vehicles in the world at any price," added *Motor Trend* editor Edward Loh, "though its price is well within reach of the average consumer."

CHAPTER ELEVEN

DRIVEN

The sixth-generation Chevrolet Camaro is ready to find new roads even as Camaro looks to the past—in March 2016, GM released the first photos of the 2017 Camaro 50th Anniversary Edition. *GM*

Sixth-generation Chevrolet Camaros are ready to depart the GM headquarters in downtown Detroit as they launch the Find New Roads Trip. *GM*

When an automaker launches a new product in North America, it typically whets the car-buying public's appetite by introducing the vehicle first to the automotive media—that is, reporters and writers for newspapers, television and radio stations, and websites—in addition to bloggers and social media influencers, anyone who can spread the word about the new vehicle.

Introductions to the media usually take place in two stages. First there is the "long lede." Monthly magazines need several weeks, even a month or two, to report, write, edit, print, and distribute their stories. For this reason, "buff books" are invited to hear from car designers and engineers in person, then they get a chance to drive the vehicle. The only caveat is that they must abide by the embargo date set by the automaker, holding their stories until that date.

The embargo date usually coincides with the second stage of the vehicle's introduction, the "short lede." While the long lede may be limited to a half-dozen publications, the short lede often includes as many as 150 reporters, brought to a location—often a swanky resort in a gorgeous setting—to hear about and to engage with the new vehicle. They spend part of a day driving the vehicle on a specified route, one that's designed to show the best attributes of the vehicle.

New Camaros roll out on the start of the Find New Roads Trip. *GM*

"THE FIND NEW ROADS TRIP STARTED IN DETROIT, WITH NEARLY TWO DOZEN OF THE NEW, SIXTH-GENERATION CAMARO COUPES, V-8S AND V-6S, MANUAL AND AUTOMATIC TRANSMISSIONS."

Timing for magazine publications called for a traditional long lede media rollout for the sixth-generation Chevrolet Camaro to be held just west of Detroit. But General Motors felt that this was a special car: built in the United States on a new platform, with new powertrain options—and even a convertible top that can deploy and retract at nearly 30 miles per hour—the car deserved a bigger media launch. Because the car was set to break the traditional development mold, so, too, should the rollout. For this reason, GM planned a unique short lede.

Except, in the Camaro's case, the short lede was anything but short.

A Logistical Nightmare

One day in late summer 2015, a brainstorming session took place in a small conference room at General Motors headquarters on the Detroit riverfront. Monte Doran—the GM public relations staffer who handles media relations for performance cars (Corvette, Camaro)—and Tara Stewart Kuhnen—an employee of the PR agency that supports GM's programs—were developing ideas for the Gen 6 Camaro short lede. One of them remembered seeing a map drawn up by a geography graduate student at Michigan State University who had created a computer program to map out the shortest driving route that included each of the lower 48 states. The other remembered that 2015 marked the 48th anniversary of Camaro production.

Maybe, they thought, we could organize a short lede for the automotive media to drive the new Camaro in all 48 states.

It was a ridiculous idea. Such a stunt would be a logistics nightmare, beyond being nearly impossible to time correctly. However the Camaro short lede would go down, it had to be done before the cars traveled from the Lansing Grand River assembly plant to Chevrolet dealerships throughout North America. Distribution was scheduled for just a couple of weeks before Thanksgiving. The calendar for the fall—both for reporters and GM staffers—was already filling up, with events such as the SEMA Show, the Los Angeles Auto Show (a major international new car showplace), and even the NASCAR racing schedule (with several Chevrolet drivers competing for the championship).

But Doran and Kuhnen were intrigued by their ridiculous idea and by the challenge and opportunity it presented: didn't Chevrolet claim it was all about finding new roads? Why not prove the claim by turning the Camaro short lede into a Find New Roads road trip?

The idea of a Find New Roads trip quickly found its way to Alan Batey, who serves as president of GM North America in addition to being Chevrolet's global brand chief. Batey also saw the opportunity that turning the slogan into a real-world adventure; he approved the program. Over the course of a month, some 150 reporters were invited to drive in a Camaro relay to take the car to all 48 contiguous states. The Find New Roads trip started in Detroit, with nearly two dozen of the new, sixth-generation Camaro coupes, V-8s and V-6s, manual and automatic transmissions. (Keys to each car were placed in a black cloth bag, which made the version of each driver assigned to a reporter a secret until the last possible minute.)

Half would head east—to Syracuse, Boston, Philadelphia, Raleigh, Orlando, New Orleans, Dallas, Albuquerque, and Phoenix—while the other half would go west—to Nashville, Kansas City, Lincoln, Minneapolis, Salt Lake City, Bozeman, Seattle, Portland, San Francisco, and Los Angeles (just in time for the Auto Show). At each of these locations, a new group of reporters would take the wheel, challenged not to follow a specified route but simply to find new roads. They were expected to turn in their cars 36 hours later at the next city along the route.

Turning reporters loose for 36 hours was risky: with no predetermined route, each car would head in a different direction instead of following a caravan of cars shepherded by a chase vehicle bringing up the rear. The drivers were all on their own. Instead of a headquarters hotel, drivers were asked to use the Camaro's OnStar system to secure overnight accommodations along the route they had selected.

There was great risk, but, as it turned out, great reward. The reporters enjoyed the freedom to find new roads. Rather than taking pictures of their cars in the same setting as all the others, each reporter shared his or her photos of the vehicles in all 48 states.

For even greater exposure, the Find New Roads trip wasn't limited to the reporters who drove. In 16 of the cities where the cars were handed off to the next group of drivers, there were public events with local Camaro club members invited to bring their own cars to join the new Camaros for a cruise-in showcase.

Finding New Roads

While there were no set routes, participants in the Find New Roads trip were encouraged to look for places along the way known for their role in *ingenuity* and *innovation*, two of the keywords that drove the design and development of the sixth-generation Chevrolet Camaro.

What's that in the mirror? A new Chevrolet Camaro SS. *Larry Edsall*

A 2016 Chevrolet Camaro SS on Interstate 75 south of Detroit. *Larry Edsall*

Above: The 2016 Chevrolet Camaro SS amid the sculpture in downtown Columbus, Indiana. *Larry Edsall*

Right: First stop on our Find New Roads Trip: Carillon Historical Park in Dayton, Ohio. The museum on the grounds showcases future GM engineering star Charles Kettering's creation of the electric starter that replaced the dangerous hand crank. *Larry Edsall*

I left Detroit on the first leg of the western route and headed to Dayton, Ohio, the site of one of the most important innovations in automotive history.

The year was 1908. In Deeds Barn on Dayton's Central Avenue, a young engineer named Charles Kettering invented a dependable, affordable electric ignition system for motorcars. Two years later, he created the electric self-starter, which eliminated the dangerous hand-crank starter and made cars more accessible and available, especially for women.

Carillon Historical Park, located just south of the Ohio city, features Kettering's inventions, the actual Deeds Barn structure, and many other important innovations and objects— even one of the early airplanes developed by Dayton's other favorite sons, the Wright Brothers. In its time, Dayton was the Silicon Valley of the early American auto industry.

My vehicle on this trip was a 2016 Chevrolet Camaro SS that linked the 455-horsepower small-block V-8 to the rear wheels via a six-speed manual transmission. I'd drawn the keys to the SS automatic out of the bag earlier that morning. The car I had picked was

A natural cave-like cleft in the limestone rock high above the Ohio River at Madison, Indiana, seemed like a good place to park for a few photos. *Larry Edsall*

red, but I wound up driving away in a black one: a photographer friend had pulled the keys to the black car, but he wanted a color that would look better in his photos. Since color didn't matter to me—and I was eager to drive the SS with a manual gearbox—we swapped. I wasn't disappointed with my decision.

With 455 horsepower and torque to match, the car is fast. Its light clutch offers a generous, easy-to-find pickup point that makes the most of the output. Even with a digital speedometer to keep you from going too fast too quickly, the power from the V-8 just flows, pouring out as if you were opening a floodgate. A wonderful sound accompanies the forward surge down the road. The shifter is nicely positioned, and there's no interference from the cupholders, which have been moved away from the driver's right arm. You also notice—and appreciate—the soft surfaces for arms and elbows during the drive.

While the car's design restricts the view out the sides and back of the car, this is compensated by features such as blind-spot mirrors and a marvelous rear-view camera system with cross-traffic alert and rear parking assist. These features are standard with the 2SS version of the car. The rear-view camera is a huge help.

Another quibble with the back end: the opening to the trunk is a little small, but the trunk itself has 9.1 cubic feet of room and can hold more stuff than you might expect.

The new Camaro is nearly 225 pounds lighter than the comparable fifth-generation model. Increased stiffness in its chassis, improved by nearly 30 percent compared again

Breakfast break in downtown Madison, Indiana.
Larry Edsall

to the previous Gen 5 car, comes through clearly in the steering system's immediate response. The feeling is enhanced by the smaller steering wheel.

The stiff chassis also allows the suspension to work efficiently. The ride is smooth and comfortable—and with surprisingly little road or tire noise in the cabin—yet there's plenty of grip in turning and even cornering maneuvers from the staggered (wider on the rear wheels) Goodyear "summer" (high-performance) tires on which the SS Camaros ride.

While the sixth-generation Camaro SS is strong, there's nothing brutal about the driving experience. That is, until you engage a full-force acceleration that pushes you back into your seat. In most driving situations, though, the new Camaro feels more like a big sports car than a slimmed down muscle car. This model is as much a big brother to the Chevrolet Corvette as it is a successor to the Chevrolet Camaro.

From Dayton, I headed west on country roads to another place known for innovation, Columbus, Indiana. This small Midwestern town rivals the world's major cities when it comes to architecture and public sculpture. From Columbus, it was more country roads—and a detour around a bridge under repair—on the way to Madison. This place feels like a small village on the banks of the Ohio River, yet it's the largest community on the river between Louisville and Cincinnati. All of Madison's downtown seems to have been included in what is the country's largest national historic landmark, with many structures preserved from the antebellum period, before the Civil War.

Once across the river, I turned onto the U.S. Interstate amd skirted Louisville before stopping at the National Corvette Museum. It was here that a sinkhole swallowed eight cars early in 2014; the museum's response to this calamity was something of an innovation in its own right. From the museum, it was more time on the Interstate system en route to Nashville, where I completed my drive and handed in the keys.

Above: Chevy, meet Chevy: The new Camaro makes a stop at the National Corvette Museum in Bowling Green, Kentucky. *Larry Edsall*

Below: A "reflective moment" as the new Camaro visits the National Corvette Museum. *Larry Edsall*

Fortunately, I had another opportunity to find new roads in the sixth-generation Camaro. In addition to doing the first leg of the western portion of the trip, I got to do the final leg of the eastern portion and, a few weeks later, flew to Albuquerque, New Mexico, to resume my trip.

From Albuquerque, I had about 36 hours to drive home to Phoenix, where the eastern leg of the Find New Roads trip would conclude. As in Detroit, I reached into the black cloth bag. This time I pulled out the tag that entitled me to a 2LT coupe, which meant this sixth-generation Camaro would be powered by a 3.6-liter V-6 engine. Since I'd already done a long drive in the V-8-equipped SS, I wasn't disappointed, and less so when I discovered this car also had a manual transmission. Chevrolet engineers have proven that the automatic gearbox is quicker to 60 mph than the manual—at least with the V-8 and V-6, the turbo four is faster with the manual—but there's something about shifting for yourself that involves the driver in the experience. Except for driving in rush-hour, bumper-to-bumper, stop-and-go traffic, when you handle a sports car you want this kind of involvement.

I was further delighted to see that this 2LT coupe was covered in what Chevrolet calls Lemon Peel—a bright, bright yellow paint color—and had black wheels. This would be a very photogenic car, especially, I figured, in the Red Rock Wildlife Area I planned to explore. The car also had an optional audio system upgrade with Chevrolet MyLink

Tom Peters, head of GM Performance Design, was born in Albuquerque, New Mexico, but hadn't been back since childhood until his leg of the Find New Roads trip. Here he's showing the new Chevrolet Camaro to the local Camaro club. *Larry Edsall*

A 2016 Chevrolet Camaro makes a stop at the Shiprock formation in northwestern New Mexico. *Larry Edsall*

Radio with Navigation and Apple CarPlay. It also featured a heavy-duty cooling and brake package with an external engine oil cooler, larger-capacity cooling system, and four-piston Brembo front brakes.

It was interesting to hear over breakfast that none of the drivers were planning the same route. I had a plan A (long route) and a plan B (shorter route), but the distances between points of interest out West can be very long; even my short route proved to be 799.2 miles by the time I turned in the car. There was also the matter of road construction that slowed my trip in New Mexico.

Appreciating the scenery, not the innovation, was my goal for this drive. I headed west and then north from Albuquerque to Shiprock, which a web search said is a "monadnock," an isolated rock rising from a plain. Called by the Navajo people the "rock with wings," the rock resembles a clipper ship rising more than 1,500 feet above the high desert. It has wall-like dikes of black volcanic rock that run in three directions from the main formation.

From Shiprock I drove north through the city that shares its name with the formation, then on into the southwest corner of Colorado and the southeast corner of Utah along the Trail of the Ancients. I've spent days in this area before, but I wanted to make time in order to reach Monument Valley before sundown. Just on the Arizona side of the state line, this is the valley made famous in so many Western movies. As it was, I didn't reach the room I'd asked OnStar to reserve for me in Page, Arizona, until well after dark, though I suppose that was in part because of a stop I made to honor one of the most effective and innovative actions in American history, the Navajo Code Talkers. The memorial site is located, of all places, in a Burger King restaurant in the town of Kayenta, Arizona.

Yellow Camaro, red rocks, southeastern Utah. *Larry Edsall*

New Camaro finds old roads on Find New Roads trip. *Larry Edsall*

Next morning, I lingered too long taking photos of the car at Lake Powell and then had to hustle to Phoenix. Thankfully, hustling isn't a problem for the new Camaro, even with the V-6 under the hood. The engine pumps out 335 horsepower with 284 pound-feet of torque. The manual gearbox lets you use that output to its fullest measure, and the exhaust provides a very rewarding sound when you do. Again, with a V-6 version that weighs 294 pounds less than its predecessor, the sixth-generation Camaro provides dynamic responses that remind you more of a modern sports car than an old-fashioned muscle car, albeit the rare sports car that averaged 30.8 miles per gallon on our Albuquerque-to-Phoenix drive.

As this book was being prepared, I'd yet to drive the new Camaro convertible or the coupe, or convertible equipped with the 2.0-liter turbocharged four-cylinder engine, both of which were due for late spring 2016 introductions. I've seen the convertible, though. Its roofline is the same as the coupe's. The operating top is a thing of beauty, a

"THE ENGINE PUMPS OUT 335 HORSEPOWER WITH 284 POUND-FEET OF TORQUE. THE MANUAL GEARBOX LETS YOU USE THAT OUTPUT TO ITS FULLEST MEASURE, AND THE EXHAUST PROVIDES A VERY REWARDING SOUND WHEN YOU DO."

Yes, it snows in Arizona, especially on the San Francisco Peaks at Flagstaff, where Humphrey's Peak reaches to 12,643 feet above sea level. *Larry Edsall*

no-manual latch, one-button operation just like the convertible tops you see in much more expensive luxury cars, complete with a hard tonneau. This covers the top when it retracts behind the second-row seat, and the top can be put up or down while the car is traveling at 30 miles per hour or less.

The 2.0-liter turbo has gained high praise in the Cadillac ATS coupe, a car that weighs 230 pounds more than the new Camaro. Chevrolet's internal testing reports a 0-to-60 mph sprint in preproduction Camaro Turbos in 5.4 seconds and quarter-mile runs in 14 seconds flat with a top speed of 100 miles per hour.

Longtime Camaro enthusiasts might scoff at the idea of anything less than eight cylinders under the hood, but there's a whole new generation of young car buyers who have learned to appreciate small, turbocharged powerplants. Attractive not only because they're affordable—these cars can be fast and furious as well.

New Roads Are Out There

My experience behind the wheel of the sixth-generation Chevrolet Camaro at the long lede and on two legs of the Find New Roads trip totaled around 1,500 miles over the course of about five days of driving. (The 150 participants in the Find New Roads trip totaled more than 171,000 miles and took the new Camaro into all 48 contiguous states.)

While I drove Midwestern country roads, southwestern mountain byways, and interstates and freeways in both regions, others on their own journeys experienced snow in the northern Rockies, the beauty of the California coastline, various sites back

The Vermillion Cliffs along the Colorado River in northern Arizona. *Larry Edsall*

East, and (from what I read via their online posts) enjoyed lobsters in Maine and Creole cooking in New Orleans. At the stopover in Dallas, racer Danica Patrick joined chief engineer Al Oppenheiser in handing over the keys to the first—and very surprised—customer to take delivery of a new Camaro.

Now that customer, and the thousands of sixth-generation Camaro buyers to follow, can head out in their own cars, with turbo fours, V-6s or V-8s, with manuals or automatics, coupes and convertibles, to find their own new roads.

Those road trips are just beginning. For the Camaro designers, engineers, and product planners, marketing and PR teams, and others, the car's sales debut provided an opportunity to look back with pride at all the work that went into car and its launch. But it's only a brief opportunity. There's an assembly line rolling along in Lansing, a convertible and turbo yet to come, as well as a 2017 model-year update and, you can be sure, more versions, including higher-performance versions of the car coming soon to a Chevrolet dealership near you.

It seems there are many more new roads yet to be found.

SPECIFICATIONS

Sixth-Generation Chevrolet Camaro Preliminary Overview

Body style / driveline	four-passenger, front-engine, rear-drive coupe
Construction	unitized body frame, one- and two-sided galvanized steel
EPA vehicle class	coupe, convertible
Manufacturing location	Lansing, Michigan

Engines	2.0-liter turbocharged	3.6-liter V-6 inline four-cylinder	6.2-liter V-8
Displacement (cubic inches / cc)	61 / 999	53/869	18/295
Bore x stroke (in. / mm.)	3.39 x 3.39 / 86 x 86	3.74 x 3.37 / 95 x 85.6	4.06 x 3.62 / 103.25x 92
Block Material	cast aluminum with cast-in-place iron bore liners	(same)	(same)
Cylinder head material	cast aluminum	(same)	(same)
Valvetrain	DOHC, four valves per cylinder continuously variable valve timing	(same)	(same)
Fuel Delivery	direct high-pressure fuel injection	(same)	(same)
Compression ratio	9.5:1	11.5:1	11.5:1
Horsepower (hp / kW @ rpm)	275 / 205 @ 5,600	335 / 250 @ 5,300	455 / 339 @ 6,000
Torque (lb-ft / Nm @ rpm)	295 / 400 @ 3,000–4,500	284 / 385 @ 5,300	455 / 617 @ 4,400
Transmissions	Tremec TR3160 6-speed Manual (Turbo 4 and V-6)	Hydra-matic 8L45 8-speed automatic (Turbo 4 and V-6)	Tremec TR6060 6-speed manual with Active Rev Match (V-8)

Gear ratios			
First	4.4	4.62	2.66
Second	2.59	3.04	1.78
Third	1.8	2.07	1.3
Fourth	1.34	1.66	1.0
Fifth	1.0	1.26	0.74
Sixth	0.75	1.0	0.5
Seventh	–	0.85	–
Eighth	–	0.66	–
Reverse	3.99	3.93	2.9
Final drive ratio	3.27	3.27 (Turbo 4) 2.77 (V-6)	3.73

SPECIFICATIONS *continued*

Chassis / Suspension / Brakes

Front: MacPherson-type strut with dual lower ball joints, twin-tube struts and direct-acting stabilizer bar; Magnetic Ride Control with monotube inverted struts (available on SS)

Rear: independent five-link with twin-tube shocks and direct-acting stabilizer bar; Magnetic Ride Control with monotube shocks (available. on SS)

Steering type: ZF rack-mounted electric, power-assisted and variable ratio

Brakes: four-wheel disc with four-channel ABS/TCS w/ DRP

Dimensions

Wheelbase (in / mm): 110.7 / 2811

Overall length (in / mm): 188.3 / 4784

Overall width (in / mm): 74.7 / 1897

Overall height (in / mm): 53.1 / 1348

Track, front (in / mm): 62.5 / 1588 (LT), 63 / 1601 (SS)

Track, rear (in / mm): 63.7 / 1617 (LT), 62.9 / 1598 (SS)

Headroom (in / mm): 36.6 / 930 (front)

Legroom (in / mm): 42.6 / 1083 (front)

BIBLIOGRAPHY

Books

Edsall, Larry. 2009. *Camaro: A Legend Reborn*. Minneapolis, Minnesota: Motorbooks.

Flammang, James M., and Ron Kowalke. 1999. *Standard Catalog of American Cars 1976–1999*. Iola, Wisconsin: Krause Publications.

Frumkin, Mitchel J., and Phil Hall. 2002. *American Dream Cars: 60 Years of the Best Concept Vehicles*. Iola, Wisconsin: Krause Publications.

Gunnell, John. 1977. *Standard Catalog of American Cars. 1946–1975*. Iola, Wisconsin: Krause Publications.

Holmstrom, Darwin. 2007. *Camaro Forty Years*. St. Paul, Minnesota: Motorbooks.

Saward, Joe, and Joe Bamber. 1989. *The World Atlas of Motor Racing*. New York: Mallard Press.

Statham, Steve. 1998. *Camaro*. St. Paul, Minnesota: Motorbooks.

Witzenburg, Gary L. *Camaro! From Challenger to Champion: The Complete History*. Kutztown, Pennsylvania: Automobile Quarterly Publications.

Young, Anthony. 2004. *Camaro*. St. Paul, Minnesota: Motorbooks.

Zararine, Paul. 2001. *Camaro Exposed 1967–1969: Designs, Decisions and the Inside View*. Cambridge: Bentley Publishers.

Magazine

Editors. 2006. "Groovy, Baby! Detroit debuts portend a thriving 2006—with muscle cars and growing segments—to make us feel good." *AutoWeek*, January 23. http://autoweek.com/article/car-news/groovy-baby-detroit-debuts-portend-thriving-2006with-muscle-cars-and-bulking.

Newspapers

Editors. 2005. "GM CEO Wagoner faces loss of confidence." *Automotive News*, November 16. www.autonews.com/article/20051116/REG/511160709.

LaReau, Jamie. 2006. "GM racks up $4.8 billion net loss for fourth quarter of 2005." *Automotive News,* January 26. www.autonews.com/article/20060126/REG/60126001/gm-racks-up-$4.8-billion-net-loss-for-fourth-quarter-of-2005.

LaReau, Jamie. 2006. "Harris returns to head GM public relations." *Automotive News*, January 31. www.autonews.com/article/20060131/REG/60131009.

LaReau, Jamie. 2006. "Chevy Camaro will be built in Canada." *Automotive News*. August 21. www.autonews.com/article/20060821/REG/60821010/chevy-camaro-will-be-built-in-canada.

Stein, Jason. 2005. "GM posts $1.1 billion quarterly loss." Jason *Automotive News*, April 19. www.autonews.com/article/20050419/REG/504190701/gm-posts-$1.1-billion-quarterly-loss.

Websites

www.automobilemag.com
www.camaros.org/assemblyprocess.shtml
www.en.wikipedia.org/wiki/Fourth-generation_Chevrolet_Camaro
www.IMBd.com
www.vtnews.vt.edu

INDEX